EXISTENTIAL ENCOUNTERS
FOR TEACHERS

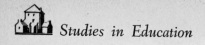 *Studies in Education*

CONSULTING EDITOR / PAUL NASH / BOSTON UNIVERSITY

EXISTENTIAL ENCOUNTERS FOR TEACHERS

Edited with commentaries by

MAXINE GREENE / TEACHERS COLLEGE COLUMBIA UNIVERSITY

RANDOM HOUSE / NEW YORK

ACKNOWLEDGMENTS

Martin Buber. Excerpts from *Between Man and Man* reprinted by permission of The Macmillan Company and Routledge & Kegan Paul, Ltd. Copyright 1955 by The Macmillan Company. Excerpts from *I and Thou* by permission of Charles Scribner's Sons and T. & T. Clark.

Albert Camus. Excerpts from *The Myth of Sisyphus* (translated by Justin O'Brien) reprinted by permission of Alfred A. Knopf, Inc. Copyright 1955 by Alfred A. Knopf, Inc. Excerpts from *The Rebel* (translated by Anthony Bowers) reprinted by permission of Alfred A. Knopf, Inc. Copyright 1956 by Alfred A. Knopf, Inc. Excerpts from *The Plague* (translated by Stuart Gilbert) reprinted by permission of Alfred A. Knopf, Inc., and Editions Gallimard. Copyright 1948 by Stuart Gilbert. Copyright © Editions Gallimard 1947. Excerpts from *Resistance, Rebellion, and Death* (translated by Justin O'Brien) reprinted by permission of Alfred A. Knopf, Inc. © Copyright 1960 by Alfred A. Knopf, Inc. Excerpts from *The Stranger* (translated by Stuart Gilbert) reprinted by permission of Alfred A. Knopf, Inc., Hamish Hamilton, Ltd., and Editions Gallimard. Copyright 1948 by Alfred A. Knopf, Inc.

Fyodor Dostoevsky. Excerpts from "Notes from Underground" from *White Nights and Other Stories* reprinted by permission of The Macmillan Company. Copyright 1945 by The Macmillan Company. Excerpts from *The Brothers Karamasov* by permission of Random House, Inc.

Martin Heidegger. Excerpts from "What Is Metaphysics?" from *Existence and Being* by permission of Henry Regnery Company. Excerpts from *Introduction to Metaphysics* by permission of Yale University Press. Excerpts from *Discourse on Thinking* (translated by John Anderson and Hans Freund) reprinted by permission of Harper & Row, Publishers, Inc.

A volume in the *Works* of Martin Heidegger under the editorship of J. Glenn Gray. Copyright © 1966 by Harper & Row, Publishers, Inc. Excerpts from *What Is Philosophy?* reprinted by permission of Twayne Publishers, Inc. © Twayne Publishers, Inc.

Karl Jaspers. Excerpts from *Man in the Modern Age* by permission of Routledge & Kegan Paul, Ltd. Excerpts from *Reason and Existenz* reprinted by permission of Farrar, Straus & Giroux, Inc. Copyright 1955 by the Noonday Press.

Franz Kafka. Excerpts from *Amerika* (translated by Edwin Muir) reprinted by permission of New Directions Publishing Corporation. Copyright 1946 by New Directions. Excerpts from "Aphorisms" from *The Great Wall of China* reprinted by permission of Schocken Books, Inc. Copyright 1946, 1948, by Schocken Books, Inc.

Soren Kierkegaard. Excerpts from *The Journals* and "The Individual" and "A Word About the Relation of My Literary Activity to 'The Individual'" from *The Point of View*, Harper Torchbooks, by permission of Harper & Row, Publishers, Inc. Excerpts from *The Sickness Unto Death* (translated by Walter Lowrie) reprinted by permission of Princeton University Press. Copyright 1941 by Princeton University Press. Excerpts from "Concluding Unscientific Postscripts" (Copyright 1941 by Princeton University Press), "Either/Or" (Copyright 1944 by Princeton University Press), "Philosophical Fragments" (Copyright 1936 by Princeton University Press), and "Works of Love" (Copyright 1946 by Princeton University Press) from *A Kierkegaard Anthology* (edited by Robert Bretall) reprinted by permission of Princeton University Press.

Gabriel Marcel. Excerpts from *The Mystery of Being* by permission of Henry Regnery Company. Excerpts from *The Philosophy of Existentialism* by permission of Philosophical Library, Publishers.

Maurice Merleau-Ponty. Excerpts from *The Primacy of Perception* (translated by Arleen B. Dallery and James M. Edie) and *Sense and Non-Sense* (translated by Hubert L. Dreyfus and Patricia Alles Dreyfus) by permission of Northwestern University Press.

Friedrich Nietzsche. Excerpts from *The Birth of Tragedy and the Genealogy of Morals* (translated by Frances Golffing) reprinted by permission of Doubleday & Company, Inc. Copyright © 1956 by Doubleday & Company, Inc. Excerpts from "Thus Spake Zarathustra" from *The Portable Nietzsche* (edited by Walter Kaufmann) reprinted by permission of The Viking Press, Inc. Copyright 1954 by The Viking Press, Inc.

José Ortega y Gasset. Excerpts from *Man and People* (translated by Willard R. Trask) reprinted by permission of W. W. Norton & Company, Inc. Copyright © 1957 by W. W. Norton & Company, Inc.

Rainer Maria Rilke. Excerpts from *Letters to a Young Poet,* revised edition (translated by M. D. Herter Norton) reprinted by permission of W. W. Norton & Company, Inc., and Insel Verlag, Publishers. Copyright 1934 by W. W. Norton & Company, Inc. Renewed 1962 by M. D. Herter Norton. Revised edition copyright 1954 by W. W. Norton & Company, Inc. Excerpts from *Sonnets to Orpheus* (translated by M. D. Herter Norton) reprinted by permission of W. W. Norton & Company, Inc., and Insel Verlag, Publishers. Copyright 1942 by W. W. Norton & Company, Inc. "The Neighbor" from *Selected Poems* (translated by C. F. MacIntyre) by permission of the University of California Press.

Jean-Paul Sartre. Excerpts from *The Age of Reason* (translated by Eric Sutton) by permission of Alfred A. Knopf, Inc. Copyright, 1947, by Eric Sutton. Excerpts from *Anti-Semite and Jew* by permission of Schocken Books, Inc. Copyright 1948 by Schocken Books, Inc. Excerpts from *Being and Nothingness* and *Existentialism* by permission of Philosophical Library, Publishers. Excerpts from *Nausea* (translated by Lloyd Alexander) reprinted by permission of New Directions Publishing Corporation. Copyright © 1964 by New Directions. Excerpts from *No Exit* (translated by Stuart Gilbert) reprinted by permission of Alfred A. Knopf, Inc., Hamish Hamilton, Ltd., and Editions Gallimard. Copyright 1946 by Stuart Gilbert. Excerpts from "The Flies" from *No Exit and Three Other Plays,* Vintage Edition (translated by Stuart Gilbert) reprinted by permission of Alfred A. Knopf, Inc., Hamish Hamilton, Ltd., and Editions Gallimard. Copyright 1946 by Stuart Gilbert. Excerpts from *The Words* reprinted by permission of George Braziller, Inc. © 1964 George Braziller, Inc. Excerpts from *The Psychology of Imagination* by permission of Philosophical Library, Publishers.

Paul Tillich. Excerpts from *The Courage to Be* by permission of Yale University Press.

Thanks are due to June Fischbein and Robert Weiss of Random House for their great help and encouragement. Gratitude is also due Professor Theodore Brameld who introduced the author to existentialist thinking in a memorable seminar about fifteen years ago.

CONTENTS

CONTENTS

CONTENTS

EXISTENTIAL ENCOUNTERS FOR TEACHERS

INTRODUCTION

To teach in the American school today is to undertake a profoundly human as well as a professional responsibility. This is a time when far more is known than ever before about the theoretical aspects of teaching and learning; but it is also a time when far less can be guaranteed, even to the student who succeeds. No longer can the teacher motivate the disinterested one by assuring him of a prosperous future if he makes an effort to learn. No longer can he motivate the sophisticated one by talking inspirationally about his potential contribution, his obligations, or the meaningful roles he will play.

This book is intended for the person who understands the problematic component in the educational enterprise. It is intended for the one who knows by now that he cannot depend on the promises which sanctioned public schooling in time past. The selections it presents have been made for the sake of the individual, teacher or teacher-to-be, who knows he must make it possible for his students to create meanings in a cosmos devoid of objective meaning, to find reasons for being in a society with fewer and fewer open doors.

The teacher in the present age is asked to undertake the rigorous task of enabling students to develop concepts in a range of subject matter fields. Only as they learn to conceptualize, he is told, can they deal effectively with the complexities of the world. And why must they conceptualize? Why must they learn to function effectively? So that they may make competent choices, the teacher is told, when they confront the situations of "real life." They are to be educated, in other words, to make their own way as persons, if not as producers; they are to be educated so that they may create themselves.

The teacher charged with such a responsibility cannot function adequately if he relies upon precedent, habit, or the dicta of authority. He must engage himself fully in his classroom life so that he can deal with each student as an individual with his own peculiar structure of cognitive capabilities. He must be ready to take the risk of making decisions without support and, frequently, without hope of justifying them in any final sense. At the very least, he must make decisions authentically and sincerely; he must take responsibility for every act which he performs.

Confronting his own freedom, his own need to choose, he is bound to suffer from disquietude. Engaged as he must be, he is bound to move into himself from time to time—exploring his own consciousness of what it is to choose, to act, to be. Whether fully aware of it or not, he is bound to be drawn to some existential mode of thinking, if only because of the work he is doing in the indifferent world.

The selections that follow have been made with such a predicament in mind. They have been taken from the writings of nineteenth- and twentieth-century existential thinkers, all of whom have been concerned with the problem of human existence in a universe barren of "sense" or sanction, concerned with the problem of freedom, with men's sometimes desperate efforts to create identities for themselves. Not explicitly concerned with schoolchildren or with schools, they have all been preoccupied with "education" in its inclusive sense: "education" as it refers to the multiple modes of becoming, of confronting life situations, of engaging with others, of reflecting, forming, choosing, struggling to be.

Encountering them, the person involved with teaching

can expect no easy answers to his questions; his doubts will not be assuaged. The existential writer, however, has a peculiar power to move the one who encounters his work to self-awareness, to confrontation of his personal predicaments, to identification of himself. The teacher who has perceived the problematic quality of what he does and who is brave enough to acknowledge what this implies needs no introduction to perplexity. He is acquainted with the disquietude in which existential thinking begins. He is already familiar with the troubling moods—of anguish, nausea, anxiety, boredom—which color experience for the one conscious of his own existence in time.

The chapters that follow, therefore, will bring him messages but not news. They will permit him to confront some of his own uncertainties; they will stir him to evaluate his commitments. Also they will provide some introduction to a philosophic stance which has aroused considerable interest among teachers: the diverse strains of thinking identified as existentialism.

Although this book has been prepared with teachers in mind, it ought not to be confused with a more general or formal introduction. No attempt has been made, for instance, to identify what are, in philosophic contexts, significant differences between rigorous phenomenologists like Martin Heidegger and "literary" existentialists like Jean-Paul Sartre. No special distinctions have been made between "religious" existentialists like Soren Kierkegaard, Martin Buber, Gabriel Marcel, and Paul Tillich and "atheist" or "humanist" thinkers like Jean-Paul Sartre, Friedrich Nietzsche, Maurice Merleau-Ponty, and Albert Camus.

Moreover, none of the many excellent discussions on existential thought have been utilized, although some are listed at the close of the book. The readings have been assembled with the specific intention of providing people in education with opportunities for first-hand encounters with men exploring facets of existence that concern those with responsibilities in the transformed world.

The readings have been organized by means of categories derived from the content of the material and considered to be of educational import: "knowing," "choosing," "the individual," "others," and "situations." The interstitial commentaries are intended as pointers, suggestions, not paraphrases or interpretations. In no case are they to be taken to represent educational statements *deduced* from the existential statements preceding or following them. The commentaries are to some degree impressionist. They suggest *possibilities* for looking at certain educational issues from an existential vantage point—but only possibilities. They are included partly to effect some kind of continuity among the selections, and partly to engage the reader imaginatively in consideration of his own commitments through the existential glass. It will be found, at the close of the book, that the commentaries, taken together, constitute a personal educational statement. This statement is to be viewed as one individual's response to the writers whose work has been selected for inclusion. The fact that that individual (the editor) is herself a teacher and deeply concerned with teaching and learning accounts for the educational content of the commentaries. If the editor were a lawyer, a government official, a painter, or a business executive, the content would have been different.

This is appropriate to the existential mode, since existential thinkers are concerned with presenting their personal responses to their own consciousness of existing. They are concerned with authenticating themselves as persons, with acting in such a way (in their case, through writing) as to realize themselves. This is quite different from the communication of doctrine, from explaining how things *are*. And it demands of the one who encounters them—as editor or reader—a move into his own consciousness, an appropriation of what is most meaningful to him, a distinctive use of what he finds.

The books from which the readings were taken all await the reader who is interested. Each one offers opportunities for more extensive experiences, more intense self-awareness to the one willing to pursue. It is hoped that the selections here will serve as lures, leading the reader beyond preliminary encounter to significant engagements with existential writers in their more completely realized domains.

The major consequence for such a reader will not be an addition to his *knowledge* about man in general, reality in general, the true, or the good. It will be a heightening of his consciousness with respect to existence as a "single one," since this is the focal existential concern.

Unlike traditional philosophers—from Aristotle to Hegel—the existential thinker refuses to conceive man as an abstraction, a category, an "essence." To describe man as a "rational animal," as Aristotle did, or to see man in Hegelian fashion as a component part of a system of "thought objectified" is, for the existentialist, to eliminate the crux: the existing individual with his own consciousness of "being," his dread of "nothingness," his need to create himself. To say that man's "essence" is his rationality is to say nothing about the existing being, with all his shifting moods, feelings, impulses, fantasies, who is struggling to cope with the world. To identify a child by giving his age group, his social class, or his IQ score is, similarly, to say nothing about the existing child in his particularity and uniqueness. To identify an individual by means of a category ("Negro," "disadvantaged," "upper class") is to give a certain amount of information; but it makes the individual, *qua* individual, "invisible"— to use Ralph Ellison's term.

The existentialist endeavors to break through such categories and essences when he considers human creatures living in the world. A physical object, a piece of furniture, a natural phenomenon may be known by means of abstractions: "table" *does* refer to a set of qualities all tables possess, and that set of qualities may be used, with certain variations, to define any table on earth. But if one says "tool-using biped," "symbol-using organism," "social animal," or even "man," one's terms in no way encompass or account for *this* person or *that* person as he actually exists.

And his existence comes first, his brute being-in-the-world. If he is to become an identity, he must plunge into action and relate himself reflectively to the situations marking his life in time. Also, he must choose. He must create values, and indeed create himself, by choosing the kind of person he is moment by moment, year by year. His essence, that which he "really" is, turns out to be the identity he defines for himself as he lives.

This is, as most existentialists see it, a subjective achievement; and they put much stress on subjectivity. Each existing person, after all, is inwardly conscious of his being. No external categorization, naming, or definition can touch that crucial awareness; each man relates himself to the world around from a perspective that is within. This does not necessarily mean that he must rely upon his non-rational capacities for "knowing." It certainly does not mean that he depends upon his unconscious mind for his existential truths.

He effects relationships with the world and with other men by means of various capacities, including reason and intuition, feeling and (sometimes) "absurd" faith. The important point is that his subjective consciousness of being alive and a "single one" is involved in whatever relationships he achieves. His consciousness of freedom —"dreadful freedom"—is also involved; since he knows that "anything is possible" for the man who cannot will himself *not* to be free. But, complementing the sense of freedom and open possibilities, is the sense of mortality, of his own personal death; and all the choices he makes and the action he takes are shadowed in some fashion by the perception of a "nothingness" which threatens a man's being and achievements every step of the way.

Perhaps paradoxically, this perception—and the moods which accompany it—makes the individual feel more sharply alive than if he believed in his own immortality, or if he denied the fact that nothing is guaranteed. From

For others, like Fyodor Dostoevsky's "underground man," the crisis was one of "consciousness," expressed in rebellion against middle-class evasions, formulas, and rules. Anger was aroused in such a man, "spite" inflamed by the sight of the ant heaps in which so many people lived, by the Crystal Palace, which symbolized invention, progress, and the security that lulled men to sleep. From a tenement on a dingy St. Petersburg street, Dostoevsky's narrator rails against determinisms and bland conformities: "What man wants is simply independent choice, whatever that independence may cost and wherever it may lead."

Friedrich Nietzsche, challenging the laziness of his contemporaries and their tendency "to think and act herd-fashion," created a Zarathustra to proclaim what was possible for those willing to break free: "A new pride taught me mine ego, and that teach I unto men: no longer to thrust one's head into the sand of celestial things, but to carry it freely, a terrestrial head, which giveth meaning to the earth!"

The poet Rainer Maria Rilke expressed a similar scorn of denial and superficiality, the same sense of the self's potentiality. "Is it possible," he asked, "that, in spite of inventions and progress, in spite of culture, religion, and wisdom, one has remained at the surface of life? Is it possible that even this surface, which would at least have been something, has been covered by an incredibly dull material till it looks like salon furniture during summer vacation?"

The problem, wrote Martin Heidegger some years later, was one of "existence" (of "standing forth") and of man who "alone exists." The problem was one of man's relationship to Being, of the threat of non-Being or nothingness; "care" was required, confrontation and concern. Jean-Paul Sartre, following after, said that man is the only "being who exists before he can be defined by any concept. . . ." Deprived of traditional categories and norms, he can no longer think of himself as a substance, an essence, a fixed identity. "Cast into the world" at birth, he is forever in a state of becoming, a condition of "dreadful freedom" to invent and create himself. "He is not ready-made at the start. In choosing his ethics, he makes himself, and force of circumstances is such that he cannot abstain from choosing. . . ."

In furnished rooms, libraries, lecture halls, cafés, and even jails, men have taken stances like these in the modern age. They have asserted themselves like this, and repeatedly rebelled. The evidence pointed to the impossibility of uniqueness and autonomy, and they defied it. Human beings, scientifically regarded, were said to be conditioned and determined in every visible dimension of their lives; and they denied that empirical or statistical study could ever encompass the "single one." Around them, individuals were being submerged in city crowds, classified, subsumed under groups and social classes; but they insisted on the possibility of subjectively experienced consciousness, of individual existence in the world.

Intensely conscious of what was happening in history, each one had suffered the experience of feeling (in Albert Camus' words) the "stage sets collapse." Each one had watched the sky grow blank and empty before his very eyes, felt under his feet the sickening slippage of old faiths. Each had undergone the realization that nothing could be taken for granted any longer: neither the rationally ordered universe, the benevolent deity, nor the traditional justifications of life.

Martin Buber explained it by saying that man once lived in the world "as in a house, as in a home," but that he now lived "in the world as in an open field." No longer secure, he had become a stranger and solitary, as if "the original contract between the universe and man" had been dissolved. When this feeling of rootlessness was coupled with a sense of being oppressed and overwhelmed by society's vast, impersonal institutions, the consequence was "nausea," or nostalgia, "homesickness" for the certainties of the past. Or there was anxiety, the "dread" evoked by the threat of "non-being," of potentialities unrealized. The existential response has been to confront the inevitability of such feelings and moods, to *live* them as aspects of the human condition. It has been to confront "absurdity" as well, the gulf between the desire for justifications and the "muteness of the universe." And what follows from such confrontation? Those who experience it may find that consciousness has been heightened by means of it, that they feel more intensely, more rebelliously alive.

They have, more often than not, committed themselves to creating the meanings men once conceived to be "given." They have defined and acted upon visions of possibility for the creature "cast into the world." They have become rebels on behalf of order and reflectiveness; and, because they have, they have had something significant to say to those at work in the schools.

AMERICAN REVERBERATIONS

And some American teachers have heard and heeded them. But when they listen, when they become interested enough to incorporate existential terminology into their ordinary discourse, they are not usually acting in response to personally experienced crises like those described by Kierkegaard, Dostoevsky, Sartre, or Camus. They borrow concepts like "authenticity," "project," "encounter," and "becoming." They weave them into the structures of their thought. As in the case of certain modern novelists, they appear convinced of the legitimacy of certain existential responses, even if they have not been particularly aware of them in themselves.

Recent works by sociologists and psychologists have impressed upon many minds the importance of "alienation" in today's society. Everyone who reads is familiar with such notions as "lonely crowd," "invisible poor," "uncommitted," and "growing up absurd." Nausea, boredom, and the sense of meaninglessness are so frequently expressed by modern artists (and by modern youth) that teachers, occasionally in negation of their own experience, have become accustomed to hearing that individuals now find it abysmally difficult to lead good lives in the corporate world. Reports of rebellion against the "establishment" and the "IBM card" abound. The evident increase in cognitive skill and organized knowledge has not appeared to help young Americans find answers to the existential "why?" nor to aid them in their searches for identity.

It is not only the wealth of current documentation which makes existentialism sound so recognizable and so "true." The themes of existential thinkers somehow recall to many teachers the ideas and commitments associated with the American Dream. They seem continuous, when first encountered, with what was said about the child in the American past, about his growing into manhood, about the bright promise of the schools.

These things were said, at first, when the advances of industry and scientific invention were being hailed as evidences of the special "progress" guaranteed to Americans. The modernization (which nineteenth-century Europeans called "Americanization") of the world was greeted by educators, as well as builders and businessmen, as testimony to the powers of the individual and confirmation of the freedom to which he was heir. The function of the schools, in such a context, was presumed to be the function of equipping young people to cope with competition, to become economically self-reliant (and thereby autonomous), to create expanding wealth of their own.

When, at the close of the nineteenth century, some of the immoralities and inhumanities of the industrial system were being exposed, when Henry David Thoreau's words about "the mass of men" were being verified, the response of the most forward-looking educators was not to decry progress nor to despair at the sight of men living "meanly, like ants," living with "hurry and waste of life." Nor was it to rebel in the face of determinisms and impersonal forces of change. It was to develop theories of education keyed to the hopes of a new Progressive Era, theories derived from a reasoned confidence in men's minds and in men's undiminished capacities to humanize the institutions they had made.

"Metaphysical despair," anguish, and rebellion were left, as they had customarily been, to the artists of America. Melville's imaginary ship's captain might destroy himself in a search for a white whale; another might struggle to create "measured forms" against ambiguity, while he sentenced Billy Budd, the "Handsome Sailor," to be hung. Mark Twain's fictional child might confront impenetrable evil on the Mississippi River banks and decide to "light out" for a non-existent "territory ahead." Fictional men and women, in the works of Stephen Crane, Theodore Dreiser, Sherwood Anderson, might be buffeted hopelessly by indifferent winds and tides and social systems and secret, stubborn needs. The actual educator, like the actual reformer, saw evil and indifference as remediable, demanding deliberate and gradual renewal, extended enlightenment rather than rebellion and despair.

Until the decade following the Second World War, few American educators showed serious concern about the plight of the individual in the modern day. John Dewey, it is true, warned that "individualism" was destroying "individuality"; but he believed this could be remedied by intelligent reform. Teachers like Hughes Mearns, Harold Rugg, Caroline Pratt, and Margaret Naumburg were eloquent about the importance of liberating the individual child from social pressures and conformities. But their interest in making creativity and self-expression possible was not an existential interest. They, too, located the evil of the world in the warping (but alterable) arrangements of society. They were convinced that, if individuality were released in the young, society and the world itself would be remade.

The "natural" seemed to most of these educators to be the source of creative energy and amenable to human control. Freedom did not seem "dreadful," so long as individuals were allowed to be themselves. The darkness —presented, for instance, in Ernest Hemingway's *In Our*

Time—and the wounds to which the young are vulnerable did not appear in educational talk. Nor did the "foul dust" F. Scott Fitzgerald perceived in America, the forces transforming the dream of rationality and heavenly cities into a dream of "raw and meretricious beauty," money, and success.

So long as the traditional confidence prevailed, existentialism was irrelevant to the educational concern. The existential thinker, after all, was reacting to "absurdity," to domains of experience where there could be no effective controls. He was responding to felt ambiguities and silences, to a "darkness" that critical thinking could only graze. Moreover, he was rebelling against the notion of the "ready-made" individual; and the oldest American commitment was defined by an essence, by an abstract vision of a free, perfectible, rational man.

What then has changed? What accounts for the rise of interest in existential thinking—for the surprising tendency of many educators to think existentially themselves? It may be that many of those who perceive significance in this point of view are reading in what they themselves have always believed. But it seems also to be the case that numerous teachers in America have been feeling the ancestral confidence—in mind, in individual potency— somehow drain away. They have faced apathy and withdrawal in their classrooms; they have felt the disenchantment of children who cannot "believe." They have been asked to govern their curriculum planning with considerations of "national policy" rather than through consultation of the requirements of the individual child. They have administered countless tests; they have grouped and classified in ever more elaborate categories. They have become aware of moral ambiguities and the rejection of traditional codes.

They have seen drop-outs, "cop-outs," rebels against the establishment, without and with a cause. They have seen youngsters take heroic risks in what have turned out to be Freedom Schools for themselves. They have found the social scientists' descriptions reinforced by the novels they have read; they have watched their students identify with Holden Caulfield, or with Jack in *Lord of the Flies,* or with Yossarian in *Catch-22.* They have listened to "hip" language and other secret languages, read scrawled messages in the subways and buses which were like cries of despair.

Not surprisingly, some have suspected their pupils to be like J. D. Salinger's Teddy in the story of that name —Teddy, who wanted a wholly different sort of school:

"I think I'd first just assemble all the children together and show them how to meditate. I'd try to show them how to find out who they *are,* not just what their names are and things like that . . . I guess even before that, I'd get them to empty out everything their parents and everybody ever told them . . ."

Teddy identifies inauthenticity and abstraction in his society with the adults who demand that young people expect the world to look the way it has always looked, "*your* way—instead of some other way that may be just as good, and maybe much better . . ."

The teacher who perceives this is the one likely to be receptive to talk of passion, subjectivity, and becoming. Such a teacher knows that (in the words of Mrs. Loman at the end of *Death of a Salesman*) "attention must be paid." Young people must be enabled to invent identities for themselves in an open world, without viable patterns, models, guarantees. They must be helped to overcome incipient nihilism, to create meanings by which to live. They must be given the opportunity to discover what Albert Camus once wrote in a Notebook:

We must take into consideration the awareness of our exile which we have suddenly acquired. The intelligence is not in confusion because knowledge has turned the world upside down. It is in confusion because it cannot come to terms with this upheaval. It has not "got used to this idea." Let it once get used to it and the confusion will disappear. There will remain only the upheaval and the lucid knowledge that the mind has of it. There is a whole civilization to be remade.

This book is addressed to those who have chosen to remake by means of education. It offers encounters to those who can take the risks of becoming and to those who can affirm the responsibility of creating themselves as teachers. The possibilities are limitless; each person must choose his own.

The learner begins in the formless and inchoate; and, in order to learn, in order to be, he must struggle against blankness and inertia, and commit himself to his "fundamental project," which is the achievement of his full human reality. To do this, he must be conscious of himself as a responsible individual, not an instance of some universal, nor yet a mere member of a group.

SOREN KIERKEGAARD

Concluding Unscientific Postscript

Persistent striving is the ethical life view of the existing subject. This striving must not be understood metaphysically; nor indeed is there any individual who exists metaphysically. One might set up an opposition between finality and the persistent striving after truth; but this would be a misunderstanding in the metaphysical sphere. In the ethical sense, on the contrary, the persistent striving represents the consciousness of being an existing individual: the constant learning is the expression for this incessant realization, in no moment complete as long as the subject is in existence; the subject is aware of this fact, and hence is not deceived. But Greek philosophy always had a relation to Ethics. Hence it was not imagined that the principle of always being a learner was a great discovery, or the enthusiastic enterprise of a particularly distinguished individual; for it was neither more nor less than the realization that a human being is an existing individual, which it constitutes no great merit to be aware of, but which it is thoughtless to forget. . . . Being an individual man is a thing that has been abolished, and every speculative philosopher confuses himself with humanity at large, whereby he becomes something infinitely great —and at the same time nothing at all. He confounds himself with humanity in sheer distraction of mind, just as the opposition press uses the royal "we," and sailors say: "devil take me!" But when a man has indulged in oaths for a long time, he returns at last to the simple utterance, because all swearing is self-nugatory; and when one discovers that every street urchin can say "we," one perceives that it means a little more, after all, to be a particular individual. And when one finds that every basement-dweller can play the game of being humanity, one learns at last that being purely and simply a human being is a more significant thing than playing the society game in this fashion. And one thing more. When a basement-dweller plays this game everyone thinks it ridiculous; and yet it is equally ridiculous for the greatest man in the world to do it. And one may very well permit oneself to laugh at him for this, while still entertaining a just and proper respect for his talents and his learning and so forth.

It is difficult, however, in a day of mass communications, city living, and systematization, to experience oneself as a separate and autonomous being. Yet, if a student is submerged—or submerges himself—in a class, a category, or even a privileged (or underprivileged) minority, he ceases to learn. He can only learn if he feels responsible for becoming, for achieving himself. This means that whatever membership he chooses for himself, be it in a peer group, a club, an organization, or society at large, must not obliterate his sense of his own uniqueness and re-

sponsibility. As a mere cog, a cypher, he will not learn: "for a 'crowd' is the untruth."

The Individual

There is a view of life which conceives that where the crowd is, there also is the truth, and that in truth itself there is need of having the crowd on its side. There is another view of life which conceives that wherever there is a crowd there is untruth, so that (to consider for a moment the extreme case), even if every individual, each for himself in private, were to be in possession of the truth, yet in case they were all to get together in a crowd —a crowd to which any sort of *decisive* significance is attributed, a voting, noisy, audible crowd—untruth would at once be in evidence.

For a "crowd" is the untruth. In a godly sense, it is true eternally, Christianly, as St. Paul says, that "only one attains the goal"—which is not meant in a comparative sense, for comparison takes others into account. It means that every man can be that one, God helping him therein—but only one attains the goal. And again this means that every man should be chary about having to do with "the others," and essentially should talk only with God and with himself—for only one attains the goal. And again this means that man, or to be a man, is akin to deity.—In a worldly and temporal sense, it will be said by the man of bustle, sociability, and amicableness, "How unreasonable that only one attains the goal; for it is far more likely that many, by the strength of united effort, should attain the goal; and when we are many success is more certain and it is easier for each man severally." True enough, it is far more *likely*; and it is true also with respect to all earthly and material goods. If it is allowed to have its way, this becomes the only true point of view, for it does away with God and eternity and man's kinship with deity. It does away with it or transforms it into a fable, and puts in its place the modern (or, we might rather say, the old pagan) notion that to be a man is to belong to a race endowed with reason, to belong to it as a specimen, so that the race or species is higher than the individual, which is to say that there are no more individuals but only specimens.

. . . A crowd—not this crowd or that, the crowd now living or the crowd long deceased, a crowd of humble people or of superior people, of rich or of poor, &c.—a crowd in its very concept is the untruth, by reason of the fact that it renders the individual completely impenitent and irresponsible, or at least weakens his sense of responsibility by reducing it to a fraction.

. . . No, when it is a question of a single individual man, then is the time to give expression to the truth by showing one's respect for what it is to be a man; and if perhaps it was, as it is cruelly said, a poor wretch of a man, then the thing to do is to invite him into the best room, and one who possesses several voices should use the kindest and most friendly. That is truth. If on the other hand there were an assemblage of thousands or more and the truth was to be decided by ballot, then this is what one should do (unless one were to prefer to utter silently the petition of the Lord's Prayer, "Deliver us from evil"): one should in godly fear give expression to the fact that the crowd, regarded as a judge over ethical and religious matters, is untruth, whereas it is eternally true that every man can be the *one*. This is truth.

The crowd is untruth. Therefore was Christ crucified, because, although He addressed himself to all, He would have no dealings with the crowd, because He would not permit the crowd to aid him in any way, because in this regard He repelled people absolutely, would not found a party, did not permit balloting, but would be that He is, the Truth, which relates itself to the individual.— And hence every one who truly would serve the truth is *eo ipso*, in one way or another, a martyr. If it were possible for a person in his mother's womb to make the decision to will to serve the truth truly, then, whatever his martyrdom turns out to be, he is *eo ipso* from his mother's womb a martyr. For it is not so great a trick to win the crowd. All that is needed is some talent, a certain dose of falsehood, and a little acquaintance with human passions. But no witness for the truth (Ah! and that is what every man should be, including you and me) —no witness for the truth dare become engaged with the crowd. The witness for the truth—who naturally has nothing to do with politics and must above everything else be most vigilantly on the watch not to be confounded with the politician—the God-fearing work of the witness for the truth is to engage himself if possible with all, but always individually, talking to every one severally on the streets and lanes, in order to disintegrate the crowd, or to talk even to the crowd, though not with the intent of forming a crowd, but rather with the hope that one or another individual might return from this assemblage and become a single individual. On the other hand the "crowd," when it is treated as an authority and its judgement regarded as the final judgement, is detested by the witness for the truth more heartily than a maiden of good morals detests the public dance-floor; and he who addresses the crowd as the supreme authority is regarded by him as the tool of the untruth. For (to repeat what I have said) that which in politics or in similar fields may be justifiable, wholly or in part, becomes untruth when it is transferred to the intellectual, the spiritual, the religious fields. . . .

. . . The crowd, in fact, is composed of individuals; it must therefore be in every man's power to become what he is, an individual. From becoming an individual, no one, no one at all, is excluded, except he who excludes himself by becoming a crowd. To become a crowd, to collect a crowd about one, is on the contrary to affirm the distinctions of human life. The most well-meaning person who talks about these distinctions can easily offend an individual. But then it is not the crowd which possesses power, influence, repute, and mastery over men;

but it is the invidious distinctions of human life which despotically ignore the single individual as weak and impotent, which in a temporal and worldly interest ignore the eternal truth—the single individual.

Just as Kierkegaard's conception of the individual is not solely a "spiritual" conception, so it is not a notion of the individual qua "rational man" alone. His effort to make clear what he had in mind was a response to the many depersonalizing consequences of modernization and urbanization, consequences many public school teachers are just beginning to perceive.

A Word About the Relation of My Literary Activity to "The Individual"

If this matter of "that individual" were a trifle to me, I could let it drop; indeed, I should be delighted to do so and should be ashamed if I were not willing to do it with the most obliging alacrity. But such is far from being the case. For me—not personally, but as a thinker—this matter of the individual is the most decisive thing. So then the only possibility left is to remove the misunderstanding. If I could succeed in making it evident to the individuals that it truly is no trifle, then in that case the disagreement also would be removed. For what occasions the confusion is the fact that people regard it as a trifle —and then are indignant that I should attach so much importance to a trifle. One of two things therefore: either the others are right about its being a trifle, and I ought to give it up; or it is, as I understand it, something very essential, and so there is no ground for complaining that I attach so much importance to something that is essentially important. Once upon a time (in a little article . . . in the *Fatherland*) I let the thing be carried as far as possible in the direction of singularity—verily not out of queer singularity on my part. On the contrary, the significance of what I did was clear to me in the highest degree, and I acted responsibly, with a full sense of my responsibility for doing what it would have been irresponsible of me not to do. I let that be done (and had it printed in a newspaper, moreover, and in an article moreover which touched upon the beginning and the end of the town gossip) because it seemed to me important to get attention provokingly fixed upon that point, which is something one does not accomplish by ten books which develop the doctrine of the individual, nor in ten lectures which deal with it, but accomplishes it in these times only by getting the laughter aimed at one, by making people a bit angry so as to make them upbraid one again and again and without ceasing for that very thing which one would wish to have emphatically accentuated and, if possible, brought to the attention of all. This is absolutely the surest sort of tutorial coaching. But any one who desires to accomplish anything must know the age in which he lives and then have courage to encounter the danger of employing the surest means.

. . . Every serious person who has any eye for the conditions of our time will easily perceive how important it is to make a profound effort and a rigorously consistent one, which does not draw back from the extreme consequences of the truth, to oppose boldly the immoral confusion which, philosophically and socially, tends to demoralize "the individual" by means of "mankind" or a fantastical notion of society; a confusion which proposes to teach ungodly contempt for that which is the prime condition of religiousness, namely, to be a single individual man. This confusion can only be opposed by making men if possible single individuals—yet after all every man is a single individual! Every serious person who knows what edification is—every one, whether he be high or low, wise or simple, man or woman, every one who has felt himself edified and God brought near to him—will unconditionally agree with me that it is impossible to edify or be edified *en masse*, even more impossible than to be 'in love *en quatre*' or *en masse*. Edification, even more expressly than love, is related to

the individual. The individual—not in the sense of the
specially distinguished or the specially gifted individual,
but the individual in the sense in which every man, absolutely every man, can be and should be, should take
pride in being, but verily will also discover his blessed-
ness in being . . . an individual. . . .

*In Leo Tolstoy's short story "The Death of Ivan Ilyitch,"
the central character is a "comme il faut" and successful
member of the Russian Court of Justice, who becomes an
"individual" only when he is told he has cancer and is
doomed to die. The difference between an "individual"
and the man who considers himself (or is considered)
what Kierkegaard called a "specimen" is communicated
directly by this passage from the story.*

LEO TOLSTOY

The Death of Ivan Ilyitch

The syllogism he had learnt from Kiezewetter's Logic:
"Caius is a man, men are mortal, therefore Caius is mortal," had always seemed to him correct as applied to
Caius, but certainly not as applied to himself. That Caius
—man in the abstract—was mortal, was perfectly correct, but he was not Caius, not an abstract man, but a
creature quite, quite separate from all others. He had
been little Ványa, with a mamma and a papa, with
Mitya and Volódya, with the toys, a coachman and a
nurse, afterwards with Kátenka, and with all the joys,
griefs, and delights of childhood, boyhood, and youth.
What did Caius know of the smell of that striped leather
ball Ványa had been so fond of? Had Caius kissed his
mother's hand like that, and did the silk of her dress
rustle so for Caius? Had he rioted like that at school
when the pastry was bad? Had Caius been in love like
that? Could Caius preside at a session as he did? "Caius

really was mortal, and it was right for him to die; but for me, little Ványa, Ivan Ilyitch, with all my thoughts and emotions, it's altogether a different matter. It cannot be that I ought to die. That would be too terrible."

Tolstoy thus communicates not only an awareness of the gulf between Man as "essence" and man as existing in time, but a sense of how the consciousness of his death may give a man an intense and inward awareness of himself.

This is one of the themes pursued by Martin Heidegger in his account of Dasein, which is being-in-the-world or the involvement with his own world by the existing person. A word as important as "Dasein" is "facticity," which is impossible to render by means of a simpler term. In Sartre's writing, as well as in Heidegger's, it refers to the dependence of the free, authentic self upon the self caught up in its relationships with objects, tools, other people—"the world." The contingency of the "for-itself" (the free, realized self) and its continual involvement with the brute, impersonal factuality of things is the self's "facticity." We shall find the point repeatedly made that the actualization of the person takes place by means of tension. This tension is due to facticity. For the existential thinker, pure consciousness is an impossibility; the existing, conscious being strives to be "for-itself" in an unending struggle to separate from "being-in-the-world."

MARTIN HEIDEGGER

What Is Metaphysics?

In dread we are "in suspense" . . . Or, to put it more precisely, dread holds us in suspense because it makes what-is-in-totality slip away from us. Hence we too, as existents in the midst of what-is, slip away from ourselves along with it. For this reason it is not "you" or "I" that has the uncanny feeling, but "one." In the trepidation of this suspense where there is nothing to hold on to, pure *Da-sein* is all that remains. . . .

With this key-mood of dread, therefore, we have reached that event in our *Da-sein* which reveals Nothing, and which must therefore be the starting-point of our enquiry. . . .

"Nothing" is revealed in dread, but not as something that "is." Neither can it be taken as an object. . . . Nothing is revealed in and through dread, yet not again in the sense that Nothing appears as if detached and apart from what-is-in-totality when we have that "uncanny" feeling. We would say rather: in dread Nothing functions as if *at one with* what-is-in-totality. What do we mean by "at one with?" . . . What happens is that Nothing shows itself as essentially belonging to what-is while this is slipping away in totality. . . .

Only on the basis of the original manifestness of Nothing can our human *Da-sein* advance towards and enter into what-is. But insofar as *Da-sein* naturally relates to what-is, as that which it is not and which itself is, Da-sein *qua Da-sein* always proceeds from Nothing as manifest. *Da-sein* means *being projected into* Nothing. . . . Were *Da-sein* not, in its essential basis, transcendent, that is to say, were it not projected from the start into Nothing, it could never relate to what-is, hence could have no self-relationship.

Without the original manifest character of Nothing there is no self-hood and no freedom. . . .

But now we must voice a suspicion which has been withheld far too long already. If it is only through "projecting into Nothing" that our *Da-sein* relates to what-is, in other words, has any existence, and if Nothing is only made manifest originally in dread, should we not have to be in a continual suspense of dread in order to exist at all? Have we not, however, ourselves admitted that this original dread is a rare thing? But above all, we all exist and are related to actualities which we ourselves are not and which we ourselves are—without this dread. . . .

Yet what do we mean when we say that this original dread only occurs in rare moments? . . . that as far as we are concerned . . . Nothing is always distorted out of its original state . . . by the fact that in one way or another we completely lose ourselves in what-is. The more we turn to what-is in our dealings the less we allow it to slip away, and the more we turn aside from Nothing. But all the more certainly do we thrust ourselves into the open superficies of existence . . .

The dread felt by the courageous cannot be contrasted with the joy or even the comfortable enjoyment of a peaceable life. It stands—on the hither side of all contrasts—in secret union with the serenity and gentleness of creative longing.

Original dread can be awakened in *Da-sein* at any time. It need not be awakened by any unusual occurrence. . . . It is always on the brink, yet only seldom does it take the leap and drag us with it into the state of suspense. . . .

To be ready to learn is to be ready for a leap, and dread is a prerequisite for pulling away from the surfaces of what-is and beginning to choose possibility. A person is most fully himself when he is aware of the limits of possibility; also, he is overtaken by guilt when he becomes aware of possibility unchosen or unrealized. What is not chosen is a negation; and a feeling of bad conscience may be experienced in a learning situation when a learner refuses to tolerate suspense, to overcome inertia and to strive. There is a kind of sinfulness in the refusal to become. But how does one become? How does one lurch into self-creation—achieve authentic reality?

RAINER MARIA RILKE

Letters to a Young Poet, No. 8

. . . We have already had to rethink so many of our concepts of motion, we will also gradually learn to realize that that which we call destiny goes forth from within people, not from without into them. Only because so many have not absorbed their destinies and transmuted them within themselves while they were living in them, have they not recognized what has gone forth out of them; it was so strange to them that, in their bewildered fright, they thought it must only just then have entered into them, for they swear never before to have found anything like it in themselves. As people were long mistaken about the motion of the sun, so they are even yet mistaken about the motion of that which is to come. The future stands firm, dear Mr. Kappus, but we move in infinite space.

How should it not be difficult for us?

And to speak of solitude again, it becomes always clearer that this is at bottom not something that one can take or leave. We *are* solitary. We may delude ourselves and act as though this were not so. That is all. But how much better it is to realize that we are so, yes, even to begin by assuming it. We shall indeed turn dizzy then; for all points upon which our eye has been accustomed to rest are taken from us, there is nothing near any more and everything far is infinitely far. A person removed from his own room, almost without preparation and transition, and set upon the height of a great mountain range, would feel something of the sort: an unparalleled insecurity, an abandonment to something inexpressible would almost annihilate him. He would think himself falling or hurled out into space, or exploded into a thousand pieces: what a monstrous lie his brain would have to invent to catch up with and explain the state of his senses! So for him who becomes solitary all distances, all measures change; of these changes many take place suddenly, and then, as with the man on the mountaintop, extraordinary imaginings and singular sensations arise that seem to grow out beyond all bearing. But it is necessary for us to experience *that* too. We must assume our existence as *broadly* as we in any way can; everything, even the unheard-of, must be possible in it. That is at bottom the only courage that is demanded of us; to have courage for the most strange, the most singular, and the most inexplicable that we may encounter. That mankind has in this sense been cowardly has done life endless harm; the experiences that are called "visions," the whole so-called "spirit-world," death, all those things that are so closely akin to us, have by daily parrying been so crowded out of life that the senses with which we could have grasped them are atrophied. To say nothing of God. But fear of the inexplicable has not alone impoverished the existence of the individual; the relationship between one human being and another has also been cramped by it, as though it had been lifted out of the riverbed of endless possibilities and set down in a fallow spot on the bank, to which nothing happens. For it is not inertia alone that is responsible for human relationships repeating themselves from case to case, indescribably monotonous and unrenewed; it is shyness before any sort of new, unforeseeable experience with which one does not think oneself able to cope. But only someone who is ready for everything, who excludes nothing, not even the most enigmatical, will live the relation to another as something alive and will draw exhaustively from his own existence. For if we think of this existence of the individual as a larger or smaller room, it appears evident that most people learn to know only a corner of their room, a place by the window, a strip of floor on which they walk up and down. Thus they have a certain security. And yet that dangerous insecurity is so much more human which drives the prisoners in Poe's stories to feel out the shapes of their horrible dungeons and not be strangers to the unspeakable terror of their abode. We, however, are not prisoners. No traps or snares are set about us, and there is nothing which should intimidate or worry us. We are set down in life as in the element to which we best correspond, and over and above this we have through thousands of years of accommodation become so like this life, that when we hold still we are, through a happy mimicry, scarcely to be distinguished from all that surrounds us. We have no reason to mistrust our world, for it is not against us. Has it terrors, they are *our* terrors; has it abysses, those abysses belong to us; are dangers at hand, we must try to love them. And if only we arrange our life according to that principle which counsels us that we must always hold to the difficult, then that which now still seems to us the most alien will become what we most trust and find most faithful. . . .

Sonnets to Orpheus (29)

Silent friend of many distances,
feel how your breath is still increasing space.
Among the beams of the dark belfries let
yourself ring out. What feeds on you

will grow strong upon this nourishment.
Be conversant with transformation.
From what experience have you suffered most?
Is drinking bitter to you, turn to wine.

Be in this immeasurable night,
magic power at your senses' crossroad,
be the meaning of their strange encounter.

And if the earthly has forgotten you,
say to the still earth: I flow.
To the rapid water speak: I am.

The human being must experience difficulty and unease if he is to be. Kierkegaard once said he conceived it as his "task to create difficulties everywhere. . . ." Friedrich

Nietzsche challenged men to "live dangerously." Fyodor Dostoevsky's underground narrator finds it "positively ill-bred" to affirm only the "normal," "to care only for well-being." Men, he said, would never give up suffering, give up the "doubt, negation" which is "the sole origin of consciousness." Doubt, guilt, "inquietude": only as these are subjectively experienced can the learning which is becoming begin. It begins when the individual feels his "dreadful freedom" fully, when he takes responsibility for himself.

JEAN-PAUL SARTRE

The Flies

ZEUS: Impudent spawn! So I am not your king? Who, then, made you?

ORESTES: You. But you blundered; you should not have made me free. . . . I *am* my freedom. No sooner had you created me than I ceased to be yours. . . . Yesterday, when I was with Electra, I felt at one with Nature, this Nature of your making. It sang the praises of the Good—*your* Good—in siren tones, and lavished intimations. To lull me into gentleness, the fierce light mellowed and grew tender as a lover's eyes. And, to teach me the forgiveness of offenses, the sky grew bland as a pardoner's face. Obedient to your will my youth rose up before me and pleaded with me like a girl who fears her lover will forsake her. That was the last time, the last, I saw my youth. Suddenly, out of the blue, freedom crashed down on me and swept me off my feet. Nature sprang back, my youth went with the wind, and I knew myself alone, utterly alone in the midst of this well-meaning little universe of yours. I was like a man who's lost his shadow. And there was nothing left in heaven, no right or wrong, nor anyone to give me orders . . . but I must blaze my trail. For I, Zeus, am a man, and every man must find out his own way. Nature abhors man, and you too, god of gods, abhor mankind. . . . You are God and I am free; each of us is alone, and our anguish is akin. Human life begins at the far side of despair. . . .

Being and Nothingness

What form does this consciousness of freedom assume? In freedom the human being *is* his own past (as also his own future) in the form of nihilation. If our analysis has not led us astray, there ought to exist for the human being, in so far as he is conscious of being, a certain mode of standing opposite his past and his future, as being both this past and this future and as not being them. We shall be able to furnish an immediate reply to this question; it is in anguish that man gets the consciousness of his freedom, or if you prefer, anguish is the mode of being of freedom as consciousness of being; it is in anguish that freedom is, in its being, in question for itself.

Kierkegaard describing anguish in the face of what one lacks characterizes it as anguish in the face of freedom. But Heidegger, whom we know to have been greatly influenced by Kierkegaard, considers anguish instead as the apprehension of nothingness. These two descriptions of anguish do not appear to us contradictory; on the contrary the one implies the other.

First we must acknowledge that Kierkegaard is right; anguish is distinguished from fear in that fear is fear of beings in the world whereas anguish is anguish before myself. Vertigo is anguish to the extent that I am afraid not of falling over the precipice, but of throwing myself over. A situation provokes fear if there is a possibility of my life being changed from without; my being provokes anguish to the extent that I distrust myself and my own reactions in that situation. The artillery preparation which precedes the attack can provoke fear in the soldier who undergoes the bombardment, when he asks himself if he is going to be able to "hold up." Similarly the recruit who reports for active duty at the beginning of the war can in some instances be afraid of death, but more often he is "afraid of being afraid"; that is, he is filled with anguish before himself. Most of the time dangerous or threatening situations present themselves in facets; they will be apprehended through a feeling of fear or of anguish according to whether we envisage the situation as acting on the man or the man as acting on the situation. The man who has just received a hard blow —for example, losing a great part of his wealth in a crash—can have the fear of threatening poverty. He will experience anguish a moment later when nervously wringing his hands (a symbolic reaction to the action which is imposed but which remains still wholly undetermined), he exclaims to himself: "What am I going to do? But what am I going to do?" In this sense, fear and anguish are exclusive of one another since fear is unreflective apprehension of the transcendent and anguish is reflective apprehension of the self; the one is born in the destruction of the other. But there also exist situations where anguish appears pure; that is, without ever being preceded or followed by fear. If, for example, I have been raised to a new dignity and charged with a delicate and flattering mission, I can feel anguish at the thought that I will not be capable perhaps of fulfilling it; and yet I will not have the least fear in the world of the consequences of my possible failure.

What is the meaning of anguish in the various examples which I have just given? Let us take up again the example of vertigo. Vertigo announces itself through fear; I am on a narrow path—without a guard-rail—which goes along a precipice. The precipice presents itself to me as *to be avoided*; it represents a danger of death. At the same time I conceive of a certain number of causes, originating in universal determinism, which can transform that fear of death into reality; I can slip on a stone and fall into the abyss; the crumbling earth of the path can give way under my steps. Through these various anticipations, I am given to myself as a thing; I am passive in relation to these possibilities; they come to me from without; in so far as I am also an object in the world, subject to gravitation, they are *my* possibilities. At this moment *fear* appears, which in terms of the situation is the apprehension of myself as a destructible transcendent in the midst of transcendents, as an object which does not contain in itself the origin of its future disappearance. My reaction will be of the reflective order; I will pay attention to the stones in the road; I will keep myself as far as possible from the edge of the path. I realize myself as pushing away the threatening situation with all my strength, and I project before myself a certain number of future conducts destined to keep the threats of the world at a distance from me. These conducts are *my* possibilities. I escape fear by the very fact that I am placing myself on a plane where *my own* possibilities are substituted for the transcendent probabilities where human action has no place.

But these conducts, precisely because they are *my* possibilities, do not appear to me as determined by foreign causes. Not only is it not strictly certain that they will be effective; in particular it is not strictly certain that they will be adopted, for they do not have existence sufficient in itself . . . their possibility has as a necessary condition the possibility of negative conduct (*not* to pay attention to the stones in the road, to run, to think of something else) and the possibility of the opposite conduct (to throw myself over the precipice). The possibility which I make *my* concrete possibility can appear as my possibility only by raising itself on the basis of the totality of the logical possibilities which the situation allows. But these rejected possibles in turn have no other being than their "sustained-being"; it is I who sustain them in being, and inversely, their present non-being is an "ought-not-to-be-sustained." No external cause will remove them. I alone am the permanent source of their non-being, I engage myself in them; in order to cause *my* possibility to appear, I posit the other possibilities so as to nihilate them. This would not produce anguish if I could apprehend myself in my relations with these possibles as a cause producing its effects. In this case, the effect defined as my possibility would be *strictly* determined. But then it would cease to be *possible;* it would become simply "about-to-happen." If then I wished to avoid anguish and vertigo, it would be enough if I were to consider the motives (instinct of self-preservation, prior fear, etc.), which make me reject the situation envisaged, as *determining* my prior activity in the same way that the presence at a determined point of one given mass determines the courses followed by other masses; it would be necessary, in other words, that I apprehend in myself a strict psychological determinism. But I am in anguish precisely because any conduct on my part is only *possible,* and this means that while constituting a totality of motives for pushing away that situation, I at the same time apprehend these motives as not sufficiently effective. At the very moment when I apprehend my being as *horror* of the precipice, I am conscious of that horror as *not determinant* in relation to my possible conduct. In one sense that horror calls for prudent conduct, and it is in itself a pre-outline of that conduct; in another sense, it posits the final developments of that conduct only as possible, precisely because I do not apprehend it as the *cause* of those final developments but as need, appeal, etc.

. . . In short, to avoid fear, which reveals to me a transcendent future strictly determined, I take refuge in reflection, but the latter has only an undetermined future to offer. This means that in establishing a certain conduct as a possibility and precisely because it is *my* possibility, I am aware that *nothing* can compel me to adopt that conduct. Yet I am indeed already there in the future; it is for the sake of that being which I will be there at the turning of the path that I now exert all my strength, and in this sense there is already a relation between my future being and my present being. But a nothingness has slipped into the heart of this relation; I *am* not the self which I will be. First, I am not that self because time separates me from it. Secondly, I am not that self because what I am is not the foundation of what I will be. Finally I am not that self because no actual existent can determine strictly what I am going to be. Yet as I am already what I will be (otherwise I would not be interested in any one being more than another), *I am the self which I will be, in the mode of not being it.* It is through my horror that I am carried toward the future, and the horror nihilates itself in that it constitutes the future as possible. Anguish is precisely my consciousness of being my own future, in the mode of not-being. To be exact, the nihilation of horror as a *motive,* which has the effect of reinforcing horror as a *state,* has as its positive counterpart the appearance of other forms of conduct (in particular that which consists in throwing myself over the precipice) as *my* possible *possibilities.* If *nothing* compels me to save my life, *nothing* prevents me from precipitating myself into the abyss. The decisive conduct will emanate from a self which I am not yet. Thus the self which I am depends on the self which I am not yet to the exact extent that the self which I am not yet does not depend on the self which I am. Vertigo appears as the apprehension of this dependence. I approach the precipice, and my scrutiny is searching for myself in my very depths. In terms of this moment, I play with my possibilities. My eyes, running over the abyss from top to bottom, imitate the possible fall and realize it symbolically; at the same time suicide, from the fact that it becomes a *possibility* possible for me, now causes to appear possible motives for adopting it (suicide would cause anguish to cease). Fortunately these motives in their turn, from the sole fact that they are motives of a possibility, present themselves as ineffective, as non-determinant; they can no more *produce* the suicide than my horror of the fall can *determine* me to avoid it. It is thus counter-anguish which generally puts an end to anguish by transmuting it into indecision. Indecision in its turn, calls for decision. I abruptly put myself at a distance from the edge of the precipice and resume my way.

The student may indeed be seen as determined by the multiple forces in his heritage and environment. He may be "explained" psychologically and sociologically; certain behaviors of his may be predicted in deliberately structured learning situations. But, after being diagnosed, described, and directed, he remains as an intentional consciousness in pursuit of being-for-itself—the full reality of himself. He remains free to act upon the possibilities he himself perceives: to choose what he lacks, to create his own being. This is his "original project"; only as he acts upon it can he, in any significant sense, learn.

Being and Nothingness

This fundamental project must not of course refer to any other and should be conceived by itself. It can be concerned neither with death nor life nor any particular characteristic of the human condition; the original project of a for-itself *can aim only at its being.* The project of being or desire of being or drive toward being does not originate in a physiological differentiation or in an empirical contingency; in fact it is not distinguished from the being of the for-itself. The for-itself is a being such that in its being, its being is in question in the form of a project of being. . . . Thus we can advance no further but have encountered the self-evident irreducible when we have reached the *project of being;* for obviously it is impossible to advance further than *being,* and there is no difference between the project of being, possibility, value, on the one hand, and *being* on the other. Fundamentally, man is the *desire to be,* and the existence of this desire is not to be established by an empirical induction; it is the result of an *a priori* description of the being of the for-itself, since desire is a lack and since the for-itself is the being which is to itself its own lack of being. . . . There is not first a single desire of being, then a thousand particular feelings, but the desire to be exists and manifests itself only in and through jealousy, greed, love of art, cowardice, courage, and a thousand contingent, empirical expressions which always cause human reality to appear to us only *as manifested by a particular man,* by a specific person. . . . Freedom is existence, and in it existence precedes essence. The upsurge of freedom is immediate and concrete and is not to be distinguished from its choice; that is, from the person itself.

The Words

As a public child, I adopted in public the myth of my class and generation; one makes use of acquired knowledge; one capitalizes experience; the present is enriched by the entire past. But in solitude I was far from satisfied with it. I could not grant that one received being from without, that it was preserved by inertia, and that the impulses of the mind were the effect of earlier impulses. Born of a future expectation, I leaped ahead, luminously, in my entirety; each and every moment repeated the ceremony of my birth; I wanted to see the workings of my heart as a crackling of sparks. So why should the past have enriched me? The past had not made me. On the contrary, it was I, rising from my ashes, who plucked my memory from nothingness by an act of creation which was always being repeated. Each time I was reborn better, and I made better use of the inert reserves of my soul for the simple reason that death, which was closer each time, lit me up more brightly with its dim light. I was often told that the past drives us forward, but I was convinced that I was being drawn forward by the future. I would have hated to feel quiet forces at work within me, the slow development of my natural aptitudes. I had stuffed my soul with the continuous progress of the bourgeois and had turned it into an internal combustion engine. I subordinated the past to the present and the present to the future; I transformed a quiet evolutionism into a revolutionary and discontinuous catastrophism. A few years ago, someone pointed out to me that the characters in my plays and novels make their decisions abruptly and in a state of crisis, that, for example, in *The Flies,* a moment is enough for Orestes to effect his conversion. Of course! Because I created them in my own image; not as I am, no doubt, but as I wanted to be.

PART II / OTHERS

*Choosing is solitary. The human being becomes himself
by transcending the immediacies of social involvement.
But he is born into a world which is inescapably communal; and other people are always present in the concrete situations which create the self in its "necessity."
Moreover, the possibilities among which the person must
choose are contingent in many ways on the social order;
and the struggle to be is in part a struggle against the
society's tendency to make an "object" out of the individual, a member of a mass, a public, or a "crowd." Finally,
the end of being-in-the-world is not the fabrication of a
disembodied self but the achievement of an identity fully
related to situations understood, transcended, lived.*

SOREN KIERKEGAARD

The Journals: 1837, 1840

It must be terrible, on the day of judgement, when all
souls come back to life—to stand there utterly *alone*,
alone and *unknown* to all, all.

. . . And just as the individual, however freely he
may develop, can never reach the point at which he
becomes absolutely independent, since true freedom on
the contrary consists rather in freely appropriating that
which is given, and consequently in being absolutely
dependent through freedom, so too with language, and

moreover we sometimes find the mistaken tendency of not wishing to accept language as the freely appropriated "given," but of giving it to oneself, whether this shows itself in the very highest regions, where it easily ends in silence (the negation of language), or in personal isolation with complete gibberish. . . .

Works of Love

Who then is one's neighbor? The word is evidently derived from "nearest," so the neighbor is the one who is nearer you than all others, although not in the preferential sense; for to love the one who is preferentially nearer one than all others is self-love. . . . The neighbor, then, is nearer to you than all others. But is he also nearer to you than you are to yourself? No, not so; but he is, or should be, equally near. The concept "neighbor" is really a reduplication of your own self; the "neighbor" is what philosophers would call the "other," the touchstone for testing what is selfish in self-love. Insofar, for the sake of the thought, it is not even necessary that the neighbor should exist. If a man lived on a desert island, if he developed his mind in harmony with the commandment, then by renouncing self-love he could be said to love his neighbor.

"Neighbor" is itself a multitude, for "neighbor" implies "all men," and yet in another sense one man is enough to enable you to obey the commandment. In a selfish sense it is an impossibility consciously to be two in being a self; self-love demands that it be one. Nor are three needed, for if there are two, that is, if there is one other human being whom, in the Christian sense, you love "as yourself," or in whom you love the "neighbor," then you love all men. But what the selfish definitely cannot tolerate is duplication, and the words of the commandment "as thyself" are exactly a duplication. . . .

"Neighbor" presses as closely as possible upon the selfishness of life. If there are only two men, the other man is the neighbor; if there are millions, each one of these is the neighbor, who is again closer to one than "the friend" and "the beloved," insofar as those, the objects of preferential love, gradually become analogous to the self-love in one. We are ordinarily conscious that the neighbor exists and that he is close at hand when we believe that we have rights with regard to him, that we may claim something from him. . . . That is, by recognizing your duty to him you readily discover who your neighbor is. . . .

But the sense of one's connection with others is not only a response to a religious imperative, not only a mode of counteracting "selfishness." It is crucial for a consciousness of self in its concreteness that the individual be able to disclose himself to another in all his particularity. But the other must be confronted in his freedom and distinctiveness, and at once as a fellow creature. This means that true communication (arising out of subjective involvement) is associated with a kind of tension, as each participant strives toward his own transcendence and liberates the other to become. The teacher, therefore, must in some manner open himself to his students in order to relate to them as free and striving beings. He must work for heightened communicability as he contends with them; but his interest must be focused upon their manifold possibilities rather than upon what is "common" to all.

KARL JASPERS

Reason and Existenz

. . . The comparison of man and animal only points to communication as the universal condition of man's being. It is so much his comprehensive essence that both what man is and what is for him are in some sense tied up with communication. . . .

Truth therefore cannot be separated from communicability. It only appears in time as a reality-through-communication. Abstracted from communication, truth hardens into an unreality. . . . In general, then, it applies to my being, my authenticity, and my grasp of the truth that, not only factually am I not for myself alone, but I can not even become myself alone without emerging out of my being with others. . . .

Community through communication is found, to be sure, already among the merely living existences; it is in consciousness as such, and it is in spirit. However, on the level of mere vitality, it can remain instinctive sympathies or interests limited to certain purposes. In consciousness as such, it can remain an unconcerned agreement upon what is correct or valid; in spirit, a deceptive consciousness of totality which however suddenly breaks off fellowship. . . .

If even the basic problem for empirical existents, which can endure only through community, is how one is to understand the other, how we can think and will the same things so that we can be actively bound together, then the authentic human essence, Existenz and reason, can nowhere be touched as deeply as by the question of its communication.

The communication of Existenz is accomplished through membership in the spirit, through the universality of consciousness as such, through proving itself in empirical existence, but also by breaking through these, passing beyond them in the loving struggle of those who will to become themselves. In contrast to the communication of identical and indifferently replaceable points of consciousness as such, this existential communication is between irreplaceable individuals. In contrast to the struggle for existence over power, superiority, and annihilation, here the struggle over the content of Existenz is without the will to power in the same sense; it is a struggle where every advance of the individual comes only if the other advances too, and every destruction of the other is my own. In contrast to spiritual community, where there is security in the comprehensive Idea, it does not overlook the crack in Being for us, and it is open for Transcendence. It expresses the inevitability of struggle in temporal existence and the inability of truth to be completed by unceasingly pushing the movement of communication forward as the authentic appearance of truth. To be self and to be true are nothing else than to be in communication unconditionally. Here in the depths, to preserve oneself would be precisely to lose oneself.

Existenz, then, only becomes apparent and thereby real if it comes to itself through, and at the same time with, another Existenz. What is authentically human in the community of reason and Existenz is not, as before in physical life, simply present in a plurality of naturally generated examples, which then find one another and bind themselves together. Rather communication seems to produce for the first time that which is communicating: independent natures which come to consciousness of themselves, however, as though they were not touched by the contingencies of empirical existence, but had been bound together eternally.

Since this occurs in historical situations which are always new, every form of Existenz which unfolds itself in communication is both the revelation of an irreplaceable (because historical) and essentially never repeatable selfhood, and also an unconditional binding together of historical men. . . .

Man in the Modern Age

True nobility is not found in an isolated being. It exists in the interlinkage of independent human beings. Such are aware of their duty to discover one another, to help one another onward wherever they encounter one another, and to be ever ready for communication, on the watch, but without importunacy. Though they have entered into no formal agreement, they hold together with a loyalty which is stronger than any formal agreement could give. This solidarity extends even to an enemy when selfhood comes into genuine opposition with self-hood. Thus there is realized that which, for instance, might exist in political parties across all divergencies as a solidarity of the best—palpable even when it does not come to open expression because there is no occasion for it or because its development is obstructed by the chances of the situation.

The solidarity of these persons has to be distinguished from the universally arising preferences dependent upon sympathy and antipathy; from the peculiar attractive force which all mediocrities exercise on one another be-cause it is congenial to them to be among those who do not make lofty demands; and from the feeble but per-sistent and passive holding together of the many against the few. Whereas all of these latter categories feel them-selves more secure because they exist as and encounter one another as masses and deduce their rights from mass-power, the solidarity of the self-existent is infinitely more assured in its personal trustworthiness even so far as the unobjectified and unobjectifiable minutiae of behavior are concerned, but is rendered insecure in the world by the weakness due to the comparatively small number of such persons and to the uncertainty of their contacts. The others, those of the mass-categories, have dozens of men as friends who are not really friends; but a member of the elite is lucky if he has but one friend.

The nobility of the self-existent spirit is widely scat-tered, the individuals that combine to form it being sepa-rated by great intervals. One who enters that nobility does not elect himself to it by an act of judgement, but enters it through the realization of his own being. The unity of this dispersed elite is like the Invisible Church of a *corpus mysticum* in the anonymous chain of friends from among whom, here and there, and through the objectivity of individual activities, one selfhood is re-vealed to another and perhaps distant selfhood. In this immaterial realm of mind there are, at any moment, a few indwellers who, entering into close proximity, strike flame out of one another by the intimacy of their communication. They are the origin of the loftiest soaring movement which is as yet possible in the world. They alone constitute true human beings.

MARTIN BUBER

Between Man and Man

The relation in education is pure dialogue.

I have referred to the child, lying with half-closed eyes waiting for his mother to speak to him. But many children do not need to wait, for they know that they are unceasingly addressed in a dialogue which never breaks off. In face of the lonely night which threatens to invade, they lie preserved and guarded, invulnerable, clad in the silver mail of trust.

Trust, trust in the world because this human being exists—that is the most inward achievement of the relation in education. Because this human being exists, meaninglessness, however hard pressed you are by it, cannot be the real truth. Because the human being exists, in the darkness the light lies hidden, in fear salvation, and in the callousness of one's fellow men the great Love.

Because this human being exists: therefore he must be really there, really facing the child, not merely there in spirit. He may not let himself be represented by a phantom: the death of the phantom would be a catastrophe for the child's pristine soul. He need possess none of the perfections which the child may dream he possesses; but he must be really there. In order to be and to remain truly present to the child he must have gathered the child's presence into his own store as one of the bearers of his communion with the world, one of the focuses of his responsibilities for the world. Of course he cannot be continually concerned with the child, either in

thought or deed, nor ought he to be. But if he has
really gathered the child into his life then that subter-
ranean dialogic, that steady potential presence of the one
to the other is established and endures. Then there is
reality *between* them, there is mutuality.

But this mutuality—that is what constitutes the peculiar nature of the relation in education—cannot be one
of inclusion, although the true relation of the educator
to the pupil is based on inclusion. No other relation
draws its inner life like this one from the element of
inclusion, but no other is in that regard like this, completely directed to one-sidedness, so that if it loses one-
sidedness it loses essence.

We may distinguish three chief forms of the dialogical
relation.

The first rests on an abstract but mutual experience of
inclusion.

The clearest example of this is a disputation between
two men, thoroughly different in nature and outlook and
calling, where in an instant—as by the action of a mes-
senger as anonymous as he is invisible—it happens that
each is aware of the other's full legitimacy, wearing the
insignia of necessity and meaning. What an illumination!
The truth, the strength of conviction, the "standpoint,"
or rather the circle of movement, of each of them, is in
no way reduced by this. There is no "relativizing," but
we may say that, in the sign of the limit, the essence of
mortal recognition, fraught with primal destiny, is manifested to us. To recognize means for us creatures the
fulfilment by each of us, in truth and responsibility, of
his own relation to the Present Being, through our re-
ceiving all that is manifested of it and incorporating it
into our own being, with all our force, faithfully, and
open to the world and the spirit. In this way living truth
arises and endures. We have become aware that it is
with the other as with ourselves, and that what rules
over us both is not a truth of recognition but the truth-
of-existence. . . .

I have called this form abstract, not as though its basic

experience lacked immediacy, but because it is related to man only as a spiritual person, and is bound to leave out the full reality of his being and life. The other two forms proceed from the inclusion of this full reality.

Of these the first, the relation of education, is based on a concrete but one-sided experience of inclusion.

If education means to let a selection of the world affect a person through the medium of another person, then the one through whom this takes place, rather, who makes it take place through himself, is caught in a strange paradox. What is otherwise found only as grace, inlaid in the folds of life—the influencing of the lives of others with one's own life—becomes here a function and a law. But since the educator has to such an extent replaced the master, the danger has arisen that the new phenomenon, the will to educate, may degenerate into arbitrariness, and that the educator may carry out his selection and his influence from himself and his idea of the pupil, not from the pupil's own reality. . . . This is almost always due to an interruption or a temporary flagging of the act of inclusion, which is not merely regulative for the realm of education, as for other realms, but is actually constitutive; so that the realm of education acquires its true and proper force from the constant return of this act and the constantly renewed connexion with it. The man whose calling it is to influence the being of persons . . . must experience this action of his . . . ever anew from the other side. Without the action of his spirit being in any way weakened he must at the same time be over there, on the surface of that other spirit which is being acted upon—and not of some conceptual, contrived spirit, but all the time the wholly concrete spirit of this individual and unique being who is living and confronting him, and who stands with him in the common situation of "educating" and "being educated." . . . It is not enough for him to imagine the child's individuality, nor to experience him directly as a spiritual person and then to acknowledge him. Only when he catches himself "from over there," and feels

how it affects one, how it affects this other human being,
does he recognize the real limit, baptize his self-will in
Reality and make it true will, and renew his paradoxical
legitimacy. He is of all men the one for whom inclusion
may and should change from an alarming and edifying
event into an atmosphere.

But however intense the mutuality of giving and taking with which he is bound to his pupil, inclusion cannot be mutual in this case. He experiences the pupil's
being educated, but the pupil cannot experience the
educating of the educator. The educator stands at both
ends of the common situation, the pupil only at one end.
In the moment when the pupil is able to throw himself
across and experience from over there, the educative
relation would be burst asunder, or change into friendship.

We call friendship the third form of the dialogical
relation, which is based on a concrete and mutual experience of inclusion. It is the true inclusion of one
another by human souls.

I and Thou

From your own glance, day by day, into the eyes which
look out in estrangement on your "neighbour" who nevertheless does need you, to the melancholy of holy men
who time and again vainly offered the great gift—everything tells you that full mutuality is not inherent in
men's life together. It is a grace, for which one must
always be ready and which one never gains as an assured
possession.

Yet there are some *I-Thou* relationships which in their
nature may not unfold to full mutuality if they are to
persist in that nature. . . . In order to help the realization of the best potentialities in the pupil's life, the
teacher must really *mean* him as the definite person he
is in his potentiality and in his actuality; more precisely,
he must not know him as a mere sum of qualities, striv-
ings and inhibitions, he must be aware of him as a whole

being and affirm him in the wholeness. But he can only
do this if he meets him again and again as his partner
in a bipolar situation. And in order that his effect upon
him may be a unified and significant one he must also
live this situation, again and again, in all its moment
not merely from his own end but also from that of his
partner: he must practice the kind of realization which
I call inclusion. . . .

*In the classroom, as in the wider world, individuals
clearly live with others, share certain agreements, engage
in cooperative action in domains ranging from baseball
to theoretical science. But living and working with others
is not the same as living authentically together. And because authentic living together can never be passive, it
involves great tension and risk. Once two beings are open
to each other, there can be a calling out of one another
into "being"; but there can also be exploitation of one by
the other, the tendency to "look" coldly and from without, to make the other feel himself to be an object or a
thing.*

JOSÉ ORTEGA Y GASSET

Man and People

But if there is to be living together, there must be an
advance from that simple state of being open to the
other, to the *alter,* which we called man's basic *altruism.*
To be open to the other is a passive thing. What is
necessary is that, on the basis of an opening, I shall act
on him and he shall respond or reciprocate to me. What
we do does not matter—I can bandage his wound or I
can give him a blow to which he answers and reciprocates
by another. In either case we live together and in reciprocity with respect to something. The form "we live"

very well expresses this new reality, the relation "we"—
unus et alter, I and the other together do something and
in doing it *we* are. If I called being open to the other
altruism, this mutual being to each other should be
called *nostrism,* or *nostrity,* "we-ity." It is the first form
of concrete relation with the other, and hence the first
social reality—if we choose to use this word in its most
usual sense. . . .

With the rock there is no *nostrity.* With the animal
there is a very limited, confused, diffused, and dubious
nostrity.

As we together live and are the reality "we"—I and
he, that is, the Other—we come to know each other.
This means that the Other, until now an undefined man,
of whom I only know, from his body, that he is what
I call my "like," my "fellow," hence someone able to
reciprocate to me and with whose conscious response I
have to reckon—as I continue to have dealings with him,
good or bad, this Other becomes more definite to me and
I increasingly distinguish him from the other *Others*
whom I know less well. This greater intensity in dealings implies *closeness.* When this closeness in mutual
dealing and knowing reaches a high point, we call it
"intimacy." The Other becomes close to me and unmistakable to me. He is not just some or any other,
indistinguishable from the rest—he is the Other as
unique. Then the other is *You* to me. Note, then, that
"You" is not simply a man, but a unique, unmistakable
man.

It is, then, within the ambit of living together opened
up by the relation "we" that the "you"—or unique human individual—appears to me. You and I, I and you,
we act on each other, in frequent interaction of individual to individual—both reciprocally unique. One of
the things that we do, and that is the most typical reciprocity and *nostrity,* is to talk. . . .

*Assuming that classroom "reciprocity" stops short of "in-
timacy" or "friendship," the teacher still must attempt to*

distinguish each individual student in his uniqueness, to avoid stereotyping or objectifying him, and—when possible—to take the "other's" vantage point toward a situation engaging them both. Impervious to that vantage point, the teacher is likely to view his students as cyphers, specimens, examples rather than as selves; in doing so, he is likely to choose himself as a kind of automaton—or a kind of stone.

JEAN-PAUL SARTRE

Anti-Semite and Jew

We are now in a position to understand the anti-Semite. He is a man who is afraid. Not of the Jews, to be sure, but of himself, of his own consciousness, of his liberty, of his instincts, of his responsibilities, of solitariness, of change, of society, and of the world—of everything except the Jews. He is a coward who does not want to admit his cowardice to himself; a murderer who represses and censures his tendency to murder without being able to hold it back, yet who dares to kill only in effigy or protected by the anonymity of the mob; a malcontent who dares not revolt from fear of the consequences of his rebellion. In espousing anti-Semitism, he does not simply adopt an opinion, he chooses himself as a person. He chooses the permanence and impenetrability of stone, the total irresponsibility of the warrior who obeys his leaders—and he has no leader. He chooses to acquire nothing, to deserve nothing; he assumes that everything is given him as his birthright—and he is not noble. He chooses finally a Good that is fixed once and for all, beyond question, out of reach; he dares not examine it for fear of being led to challenge it and having to seek it in another form. The Jew only serves him as a pretext; elsewhere his counterpart will make use of the Negro

or the man of yellow skin. The existence of the Jew
merely permits the anti-Semite to stifle his anxieties at
their inception by persuading himself that his place in
the world has been marked out in advance, that it awaits
him, and that tradition gives him the right to occupy it.
Anti-Semitism, in short, is fear of the human condition.
The anti-Semite is a man who wishes to be pitiless stone,
a furious torrent, a devastating thunderbolt—anything
except a man.

*There are other dangers as well, perhaps not as great as
this but potentially almost as damaging. One of them
derives from irresponsibility, when the individual does
not seize the initiative in and the responsibility for his
own coming to be. Another arises out of the tension necessarily implicit in relationships in which people are
"open" to each other as subjective beings. Each one—
even in the context of an I-Thou encounter—may be so
desperately trying to assert his own subjectivity that he
fixes the other in a terrible permanence. It is as if he
affirms that the other's being has been eternally defined,
eternally confirmed—and that the other, denied responsibility for choosing himself any longer, is as if he were
dead.*

No Exit

GARCIN: . . . Listen! Every man has an aim in life, a
leading motive; that's so, isn't it? Well, I didn't give a
damn for wealth, or for love. I aimed at being a real man.
A tough, as they say. I staked everything on the same
horse. . . . Can one possibly be a coward when one's
deliberately courted danger at every turn? And can one
judge a life by a single action?

INEZ: Why not? For thirty years you dreamt you were
a hero, and condoned a thousand petty lapses—because a
hero, of course, can do no wrong. An easy method,
obviously. Then a day came when you were up against

it, the red light of real danger—and you took the train to Mexico.

GARCIN: I "dreamt," you say. It was no dream. When I chose the hardest path, I made my choice deliberately. A man is what he wills himself to be.

INEZ: Prove it. Prove it was no dream. It's what one does, and nothing else, that shows the stuff one's made of.

GARCIN: I died too soon. I wasn't allowed time to—to do my deeds.

INEZ: One always dies too soon—or too late. And yet one's whole life is complete at that moment, with a line drawn neatly under it, ready for the summing up. You are—your life, and nothing else.

GARCIN: What a poisonous woman you are! With an answer for everything.

INEZ: Now then! Don't lose heart. It shouldn't be so hard, convincing me. Pull yourself together, man, rake up some arguments. (GARCIN *shrugs his shoulders.*) Ah, wasn't I right when I said you were vulnerable? Now you're going to pay the price, and what a price! You're a coward, Garcin, because I wish it. I wish it—do you hear?—I wish it. And yet, just look at me, see how weak I am, a mere breath on the air, a gaze observing you, a formless thought that thinks you. . . .

.   .   .

INEZ: Well, what are you waiting for? Do as you're told. What a lovely scene: coward Garcin holding baby-killer Estelle in his manly arms! Make your stakes, everyone. Will coward Garcin kiss the lady, or won't he dare? What's the betting? I'm watching you, everybody's watching. I'm a crowd all by myself. Do you hear the crowd? Do you hear them muttering, Garcin? Mumbling and muttering. "Coward! Coward! Coward! Coward!"—that's what they're saying. . . . It's no use trying to escape, I'll never let you go. What do you hope to get from her silly lips? Forgetfulness? But I shan't forget you, not I! "It's I you must convince." So come to me. I'm waiting. Come along, now. . . . Look how obedient he is, like

a well-trained dog who comes when his mistress calls.
You can't hold him, and you never will.

GARCIN: Will night never come?

INEZ: Never.

GARCIN: You will always see me?

INEZ: Always. . . .

GARCIN: This bronze. (*Strokes it thoughtfully*) Yes,
now's the moment; I'm looking at this thing on the
mantelpiece, and I understand that I'm in hell. I tell
you, everything's been thought out beforehand. They
knew I'd stand at the fireplace stroking this thing of
bronze, with all those eyes intent on me. Devouring me.
(*He swings around abruptly.*) What? Only two of you?
I thought there were more; many more. (*Laughs.*) So
this is hell. I'd never have believed it. You remember all
we were told about the torture-chambers, the fire and
brimstone, the "burning marl." Old wives' tales! There
is no need for red-hot pokers. Hell is—other people!

Being and Nothingness

This woman whom I see coming toward me, this man
who is passing by in the street, this beggar whom I hear
calling before my window, all are for me *objects*—of that
there is no doubt. Thus it is true that at least one of the
modalities of the Other's presence to me is *object-ness*.
But we have seen that if this relation of object-ness is
the fundamental relation between the Other and myself,
then the Other's existence remains purely conjectural.
Now it is not only conjectural but *probable* that this
voice which I hear is that of a man and not a song on a
phonograph; it is infinitely *probable* that the passerby
whom I see is a man and not a perfected robot. This
means that without going beyond the limits of probability
and indeed because of this very probability, my apprehension of the Other as an object essentially refers me
to a fundamental apprehension of the Other in which
he will not be revealed to me as an object but as a
"presence in person." . . . The classical theories are right

in considering that every perceived human organism *refers* to something and that this to which it refers is the foundation and guarantee of its probability. Their mistake lies in believing that this reference indicates a separate existence, a consciousness which would be behind its perceptible manifestations. . . . Whether or not this consciousness exists in a separate state, the face which I see does not refer to it; it is not this consciousness which is the truth of the probable object which I perceive. In actual fact the reference to a twin upsurge in which the Other is presence for me is to a "being-in-a-pair-with-the-Other," and this is given outside of knowledge proper even if the latter be conceived as . . . on the order of intuition. In other words, the problem of Others has generally been treated as if the primary relation by which the Other is discovered is objectness; that is, as if the Other were first revealed—directly or indirectly—to our perception. But since this perception by its very nature refers to something other than to itself and since it can refer neither to an infinite series of appearances of the same type . . . nor to an isolated entity located on principle outside my reach, its essence must be to refer to a primary relation between my consciousness and the Other's. This relation, in which the Other must be given to me directly as a subject although in connection with me, is the fundamental relation, the very type of my being-for-others.

. . . It is in the reality of everyday life that the Other appears to us, and his probability refers to everyday reality. The problem is precisely this: there is in everyday reality an original relation to the Other which can be constantly pointed to and which consequently can be revealed to me. . . . In order to understand it, I must question more exactly this ordinary appearance of the Other in my field of perception. . . .

. . . The grass is something qualified; it is *this* green grass which exists for the Other; in this sense the very quality of the object, its deep, raw green is in direct relation to this man. This green turns toward the Other a face which escapes me. I apprehend the relation of the green to the Other as an objective relation, but I cannot apprehend the green as it appears to the Other. Thus suddenly an object has appeared which has stolen the world from me. Everything is in place; everything still exists for me; but everything is traversed by an invisible flight and fixed in the direction of a new object. The appearance of the Other in the world corresponds therefore to a fixed sliding of the whole universe, to a decentralization of the world which undermines the centralization which I am simultaneously effecting. . . .

. . . On this level the Other is an object in the world, an object which can be defined by the world. . . . If it is this which defines the objectivity of the Other, then to what original presence of the Other does it refer? At present we can give this answer: if the Other-as-object is defined in connection with the world as the object which *sees* what I see, then my fundamental connection with the Other-as-subject must be able to be referred back to my permanent possibility of *being seen* by the Other. It is in and through the revelation of my being-as-object for the Other that I must be able to apprehend the presence of his being-as-subject. For just as the Other is a probable object for me-as-subject, so I can discover myself in the process of becoming a probable object for only a certain subject. This revelation can not derive from the fact that *my universe is an object for the Other-as-object,* as if the Other's look after having wandered over the lawn and the surrounding objects came . . . to place itself on me. . . . A radical conversion of the Other is necessary if he is to escape objectivity. Therefore I can not consider the look which the Other directs on me as one of the possible manifestations of his objective being; the Other can not look at *me* as he looks at the grass. Furthermore my objectivity can not itself derive for me from the objectivity of the world since I am precisely the one by whom *there is* a world; that is, the one who on principle can not be an object for himself. . . .

. . . We can not perceive the world and at the same time apprehend a look fastened upon us; it must be either one or the other. This is because to perceive is to *look at,* and to apprehend a look is not to apprehend a look-as-object-in-the-world (unless the look is not directed upon us); it is to be conscious of being *looked at.* . . . What does *being seen* mean for me?

Let us imagine that moved by jealousy, curiosity, or vice I have just glued my ear to the door and looked through a keyhole. I am alone . . . there is no self to inhabit my consciousness, nothing therefore to which I can refer my acts in order to qualify them. They are in no way *known;* I *am my acts* and hence they carry in themselves their whole justification. I am a pure consciousness of things, and things, caught up in the circuit of my selfness, offer to me their potentialities as the proof of my . . . consciousness of my own possibilities. This means that behind that door, a spectacle is presented as "to be seen," a conversation as to be heard. . . .

. . . But all of a sudden I hear footsteps in the hall. Someone is looking at me! What does this mean? It means that I am suddenly affected in my being and that essential modifications appear in my structure—modifications which I can apprehend and fix conceptually by means of the reflective *cogito.*

First of all, I now exist as *myself* for my unreflective consciousness. It is this irruption of the self which has been most often described: I see *myself* because *somebody* sees me. . . . This way of putting it is not wholly exact. . . . So long as we considered the for-itself in its isolation, we were able to maintain that the unreflective consciousness can not be inhabited by a self; the self was given in the form of an object and only for the reflective consciousness. But here the self comes to haunt the unreflective consciousness. Now the unreflective consciousness is a consciousness of the world. Therefore for the unreflective consciousness the self exists on the level of objects in the world; this role which devolved only on the reflective consciousness—the making-present of the self—belongs now to the unreflective consciousness. . . . The unreflective consciousness does not apprehend the person directly or as *its* object; the person is presented to consciousness *in so far as the person is an object for the Other*. This means that all of a sudden I am conscious of myself as escaping myself, not that I am the foundation of my own nothingness but in that I have my foundation outside myself. I am for myself only as I am a pure reference to the Other.

The Other, as here conceived, always threatens one's freedom and somehow deprives one of one's possibilities. A common way of affirming oneself in encounters with the Other is by transforming him into an object, just as he transforms the self into an object by his look. This is one approach to the irreducible tension of relationships among "open" human beings. There is another as well—the approach of "inter-subjectivity."

GABRIEL MARCEL

The Mystery of Being, II

Perhaps the shortest way towards our needed definition of the notion of mystery would be to begin by working out the distinction, at the spiritual level, between what we call an *object* and what we call a *presence*. . . . We can, for instance, have a very strong feeling that somebody who is sitting in the same room as ourselves, sitting quite near us, someone whom we can look at and listen to and whom we could touch if we wanted to make a final test of his reality, is nevertheless far further away from us than some loved one who is perhaps thousands of miles away. . . . We could say that the man sitting beside us was in the same room as ourselves, but that he was not really *present* there, that his *presence* did not make itself felt. But what do I mean by presence, here? It is not that we could not communicate with this man; we are supposing him neither deaf, blind, nor idiotic. Between ourselves and him a kind of physical, but merely physical, communication is possible; the image of the passing of messages between a reception point and an emission point, which we have rejected on several other occasions, is in fact quite applicable here. Yet something essential is lacking. One might say that what we have with this person, who is in the room, but somehow not really present to us, is communication without communion: unreal communication, in a word. He understands what I say to him, but he does not understand *me*: I may even have the extremely disagreeable feeling that my own words, as he repeats them to me, as he reflects them back at me, have become unrecognizable. By a very singular phenomenon, indeed, this stranger interposes himself between me and my own reality, he makes me in some sense also a stranger to myself; I am not really myself while I am with him.

The opposite phenomenon, however, can also take place. When somebody's presence does really make itself felt, it can refresh my inner being; it reveals me to myself, it makes me more fully myself than I should be if I were not exposed to its impact. All this, of course, though nobody would attempt to deny that we do have such experiences, is very difficult to express in words; and we should ask ourselves why. The fact is that the notion of the *object*, as such, is linked in our minds with a whole set of possible practical operations ("*This* object is a typewriter, and this, and this, and this, etc. are what you do with it . . .") that can be taught and that can thus be regarded as generally communicable. But these considerations do not apply, in any sense at all, to the notion of the *presence*, as such. It would be quite chimerical to hope to instruct somebody in the art of *making his presence felt*; the most one could do would be to suggest that he draw attention to himself by making funny faces!

The whole business would be rather like teaching a woman how to have charm. . . .

. . . Though we cannot, of course, regard charm and presence as merely identical, charm does seem to be one of the ways, nevertheless, in which a presence makes itself felt. Felt, of course, by this, that, or the other specific person; felt in an atmosphere of a certain intimacy; not necessarily felt, obviously, by anybody at all who comes across our charming person at a large public meeting. And this very fact that charm, which is the expression of a presence, works in some conditions and not in others, for some people and not for others, underlines the non-objective character of the notion of presence. *Non-objective* does not, however, in our present context, really in the least mean *merely subjective,* in the privative interpretation of that phrase; it does not mean being more or less of the nature of an intermittent hallucination. Instead of subjectivity, we should think of inter-subjectivity. Charm is non-objective but it is intersubjective. However, even the term "intersubjectivity" might give rise to misunderstandings, for one might conceive of a content—still an objective content—that could be, as it were, transmitted from subject to subject. But the very notion of transmission must be excluded at this level of discourse; the communion in which presences become manifest to each other, and the transmission of purely objective messages, do not belong to the same realm of being. . . .

Just as it is possible to be an existential thinker and a scientist, so it is possible to manifest oneself as a presence while teaching "objective content" to students. It is necessary to find some alternative to "object-ness" when students are confronted ("seen") by their teacher; since, only when they are present to one another, can the learning which is becoming occur.

MAURICE MERLEAU-PONTY

The Primacy of Perception

. . . Just as the perception of a thing opens me up to being, by realizing the paradoxical synthesis of an infinity of perceptual aspects, in the same way the perception of the other founds morality by realizing the paradox of an *alter ego,* of a common situation, by placing my perspectives and my incommunicable solitude in the visual field of another and of all the others. Here as everywhere else the primacy of perception—the realization, at the very heart of our most personal experience, of a fecund contradiction which submits this experience to the regard of others—is the remedy to skepticism and pessimism. If we admit that sensibility is enclosed within itself, and if we do not seek communication with the truth and with others except on the level of a disembodied reason, then there is not much to hope for. Nothing is more pessimistic or skeptical than the famous text in which Pascal, asking himself what it is to love, remarks that one does not love a woman for her beauty, which is perishable, or for her mind, which she can lose, and then suddenly concludes: "One never loves anybody; one loves only qualities." Pascal is proceeding like the skeptic who asks *if* the world exists, remarks that the table is only a sum of sensations, the chair another sum of sensations, and finally concludes: one never sees anything; one sees only sensations.

If, on the contrary, as the primacy of perception requires, we call what we perceive "the world," and what we love "the person," there is a type of doubt concerning man, and a type of spite, which become impossible. Certainly, the world which we thus find is not absolutely reassuring. We weigh the hardihood of the love which promises beyond what it knows, which claims to be eternal when a sickness, perhaps an accident, will destroy it. . . . But it is *true,* at the moment of this promise, that our love extends beyond qualities, beyond the body, beyond time, even though we could not love without qualities, bodies, and time. . . . Just as I grasp time through my present and by being present, I perceive others through my individual life, in the tension of an experience which transcends itself. . . .

ALBERT CAMUS

The Plague

Tarrou said in a low voice that it was never over, and there would be more victims, because that was in the order of things.

"Perhaps," the doctor answered. "But, you know, I feel more fellowship with the defeated than with saints. Heroism and sanctity don't really appeal to me, I imagine. What interests me is being a man."

"Yes, we're both after the same thing, but I'm less ambitious."

Rieux supposed Tarrou was jesting and turned to him with a smile. But, faintly lit by the dim radiance falling from the sky, the face he saw was sad and earnest. There was another gust of wind and Rieux felt it warm on his skin. Tarrou gave himself a little shake.

"Do you know," he said, "what we now should do for friendship's sake?"

"Anything you like, Tarrou."

"Go for a swim. It's one of these harmless pleasures that even a saint-to-be can indulge in, don't you agree?" Rieux smiled again, and Tarrou continued: "With our passes, we can get out on the pier. Really, it's too damn silly, living only in and for the plague. Of course, a man should fight for the victims, but if he ceases caring for anything outside that, what's the use of his fighting?"

"Right," Rieux said. "Let's go."

There are many ways of thinking, many ways of relating one's self to situations. What is crucial for existential knowledge of the world, however, is the priority of consciousness, of existence. ("Sum ergo cogito": I am, therefore I think.) The thinker—or the subject—does not ask what he can know, but how he can know. He does not stand apart from the world, seen as object or substance; he tries first of all to become conscious of the way the world reveals itself to him in its lived concreteness. Not all knowledge, of course, is to be grasped immediately, in terms of what is "given" in experience; but, in order not to falsify his relationship to the world, the individual knower must begin with the disquieting consciousness of himself "in the midst of life."

FYODOR DOSTOEVSKY

The Brothers Karamasov

". . . With my pitiful, earthly, Euclidian understanding, all I know is that there is suffering and that there are none guilty; that cause follows effect, simply and directly, and that I know it—I must have justice, or I will destroy myself. And not justice in some remote time and space, but here on earth, and that I could see myself. I have believed in it. I want to see it, and if I am dead by then, let me rise again, for if it all happens without me, it will be too unfair. Surely I haven't suffered, simply that I, my crimes and my sufferings, may manure the soil of the future harmony for somebody else. I want to see with my own eyes the hind lie down with the lion and the victim rise up and embrace his murderer. I want to be there when every one suddenly understands what it has all been for. All the religions of the world are built on this longing, and I am a believer. But then there are the children, and what am I to do about them? That's a question I can't answer. For the hundredth time I repeat, there are numbers of questions, but I've taken only the children, because in their case what I mean is so unanswerably clear. Listen! If all must suffer to pay for the eternal harmony, what have children to do with it, tell me, please? It is beyond all comprehension why they should suffer, and why they should pay for the harmony. Why should they, too, furnish material to enrich the soil for the harmony of the future? I understand solidarity in sin among men. I understand solidarity in retribution, too; but there can be no such solidarity with children. And if it is really true that they must share responsibility for all their fathers' crimes, such a truth is not of this world and is beyond my comprehension. Some jester will say, perhaps, that the child would have grown up and sinned, but you see he didn't grow up, he was torn to pieces by the dogs, at eight years old. . . . Is there in the whole world a being who would have the right to forgive and could forgive? I don't want harmony. From love for humanity I don't want it. I would rather be left with the unavenged suffering. I would rather remain with my unavenged suffering and unsatisfied indignation, *even if I were wrong*. Besides, too high a price is asked for harmony; it's beyond our means to pay so much to enter on it. And so I hasten to give back my entrance ticket, and if I am an honest man I am bound to give it back as soon as possible. And that I am doing. It's not God that I don't accept, Alyosha, only I most respectfully return Him the ticket."

"That's rebellion," murmured Alyosha, looking down.

Notes from Underground

Allow me to indulge my fancy. You see, gentleman, reason is an excellent thing, there's no disputing that, but reason is nothing but reason and satisfies only the rational side of man's nature, while will is a manifestation of the whole life, that is, of the whole human life including reason and all the impulses. And although our life, in this manifestation of it, is often worthless, yet it is life and not simply extracting square roots. Here I, for instance, quite naturally want to live, in order to satisfy all my capacities for life, and not simply my capacity for reasoning, that is, not simply one twentieth my capacity for life. What does reason know? Reason only knows what it has succeeded in learning . . . and human nature acts as a whole, with everything that is in it, consciously or unconsciously, and even if it goes wrong, it lives.

None of this means that the individual ought to choose irrationalism as he lives his life. It is simply that he will feel neither his freedom nor the risks of reflectiveness if he satisfies himself with general statements and syllogistic arguments, if he stops asking the existential questions at the "boundaries" of his life. It may be, indeed, that he will never appreciate empirical truth if he does not confront the unanswerable and appropriate the rebellious "truth" of consciousness—of the world as immediately revealed.

SOREN KIERKEGAARD

Concluding Unscientific Postscript

When the question of truth is raised in an objective manner, reflection is directed objectively to the truth, as an object to which the knower is related. Reflection is not focused upon the relationship, however, but upon the question of whether it is the truth to which the knower is related. If only the object to which he is related is the truth, the subject is accounted to be in the truth. When the question of the truth is raised subjectively, reflection is directed subjectively to the nature of the individual's relationship: if only the mode of this relationship is in the truth, the individual is in the truth, even if he should happen to be thus related to what is not true.

. . .

. . . The objective accent falls on WHAT is said, the subjective accent on HOW it is said. This distinction holds even in the aesthetic realm, and receives definite expression in the principle that what is in itself true may in the mouth of such and such a person become untrue. In these times this distinction is particularly worthy of notice for, if we wish to express in a single sentence the difference between ancient times and our own, we should doubtless have to say: "In ancient times only an individual here and there knew the truth; now all know it, but the inwardness of its appropriation stands in an inverse relationship to the extent of its dissemination." Aesthetically the contradiction that truth becomes untruth in this or that person's mouth is best construed comically. In the ethico-religious sphere, the accent is again on the "how." But this is not to be understood as referring to demeanor, expression, delivery, or the like; rather it refers to the relationship sustained by the existing individual, in his own existence, to the content of his utterance. Objectively the interest is focused merely on the thought-content; subjectively on the inwardness. At its maximum this inward "how" is the passion of the infinite, and the passion of the infinite is the truth. But the passion of the infinite is precisely subjectivity, and thus subjectivity becomes the truth. Objectively there is no infinite decision, and hence it is objectively in order to annul the difference between good and evil, together with the principle of contradiction, and therewith also the infinite difference between the true and the false. Only in subjectivity is there decision, to seek objectivity is to be in error. It is the passion for the infinite that is the decisive factor and not its content, for its content is precisely itself. In this manner subjectivity and the subjective "how" constitute the truth.

. . . When subjectivity is the truth, the conceptual determination of the truth must include an expression for the antithesis to objectivity, a memento of the fork in the road where the way swings off; this expression will also indicate the tension of the subjective inwardness. Here is such a definition of truth: *An objective uncertainty held fast in an appropriation-process of the most passionate inwardness is the truth,* the highest truth attainable for an *existing individual.* At the point where the way swings off . . . there objective knowledge is placed in abeyance. The truth is precisely the venture which chooses an objective uncertainty with the passion for the infinite. I contemplate nature in the hope of finding God, and I see omnipotence and wisdom; but I also see much else that disturbs my mind and excites anxiety. The sum of all this is an objective uncertainty. But it is for this very reason that the inwardness becomes as intense as it is, for it embraces this objective uncertainty with the entire passion of the infinite. In the case of a mathematical proposition, the objectivity is given, but for this reason the truth of such a proposition is also an indifferent truth. . . . In the principle that subjectivity, inwardness, is the truth, there is comprehended the Socratic wisdom, whose everlasting merit it was to have become aware of the essential significance of existence, of the fact that the knower is an existing individual. . . .

There is a difference between the "existing individual" *(or the existential thinker) and the one who cogitates,* *infers, analyzes, describes. Each, in effect, seeks a truth* *peculiar to him—or, more properly, a truth contingent upon the method he uses in his inquiry and upon the subject matter with which he is concerned. There is no reason, however, why the same person who engages in scientific investigation and attempts to relate himself to objects (or content) in such a manner as to achieve empirical or formal truth should not also become an existing individual. As individual, relating himself inwardly to his own lived life, he can confront objective uncertainty with respect to good, bad, harmony, and the infinite; he can, like Ivan Karamasov, "rebel." But, if this is to occur, he must be given the opportunity to discover his truths —and his errors—by himself.*

Philosophical Fragments

If the Teacher serves as an occasion by means of which the learner is reminded, he cannot help the learner to recall that he really knows the Truth; for the learner is in a state of Error. What the Teacher can give him occasion to remember is, that he is in Error. But in this consciousness the learner is excluded from the Truth even more decisively than before, when he lived in ignorance of his Error. In this manner, the Teacher thrusts the learner away from him, precisely by serving as a reminder; only that the learner, in being thrust back upon himself, does not discover that he knew the Truth already, but discovers his Error; with respect to which act of consciousness the Socratic principle holds, that the Teacher is merely an occasion, whoever he may be. . . . For my own Error is something I can discover only by myself, since it is only when I have discovered it that it is discovered, even if the whole world knew of it before. . . .

. . . But one who gives the learner not only the Truth, but also the condition for understanding it, is more than Teacher. All instruction depends upon the presence, in the last analysis of the requisite condition; if this is lacking, no Teacher can do anything. For otherwise he would find it necessary not only to transform the learner, but to re-create him before beginning to teach him. . . .

The good teacher becomes an occasion for permitting a child to decide consciously on freedom and becoming. In his freedom, the child may also be enabled to distinguish among the various perspectives available to him and to adjust them to one another for the sake of wider vision and of "objectivity."

FRIEDRICH NIETZSCHE

The Genealogy of Morals (Third Essay)

It is no small discipline and preparation of the intellect on its road to final "objectivity" to see things for once through the wrong end of the telescope; and "objectivity" is not meant here to stand for "disinterested contemplation" (which is a rank absurdity) but for an ability to have one's pros and cons within one's command and to use them or not, as one chooses. It is of the greatest importance to know how to put the most diverse perspectives and psychological interpretations at the service of intellection. Let us from now on be on our guard against the hallowed philosophers' myth of a "pure, will-less, painless, timeless knower"; let us beware of the tentacles of such contradictory notions as "pure reason," "absolute knowledge," "absolute intelligence." All these concepts presuppose an eye such as no living being can imagine, an eye required to have no direction, to abrogate its active and interpretative powers—precisely those powers that alone make of seeing, seeing *something*. All seeing is essentially perspective, and so is all knowing. The more emotions we allow to speak in a given matter, the more different eyes we can put on in order to view a given spectacle, the more complete will be our conception of it, the greater our "objectivity." But to eliminate the will, to suspend the emotions altogether, provided it could be done—surely this would be to castrate the intellect, would it not?

Neither "disinterested contemplation," in any case, nor scientific investigation can provide a man with the certitude, the permanence he yearns for to relieve his doubts and anxieties. Only as he accepts his concrete life situation and works to appropriate the truth of it can he attain some sustaining sense of his own reality. He lives his life in a public world that is "given," tangible, located in time; and he must also come to know that world in its multiple dimensions. He will come to know, however, only if he asks his own questions; and he will only ask his own questions if he becomes aware of his own existence in its temporality, its "historicity."

KARL JASPERS

Man in the Modern Age

For his activities in every situation and in all occupations, man needs a specific expert knowledge concerning things and concerning himself as life. But expert knowledge alone is never adequate for it only becomes significant in virtue of him who possesses it. The use I make of it is primarily determined by my own will. The best laws, the most admirable institutions, the most trustworthy acquirements of knowledge, the most effective technique, can be used in conflicting ways. They are of no avail unless individual human beings fulfill them with an effective and valuable reality. What actually happens, therefore, cannot be modified merely by an improvement in expert knowledge; only through man's being can it be decisively altered. Decisive is a man's inward attitude, the way in which he contemplates his world and grows aware of it, the essential value of his satisfactions—these things are the origin of what he does.

Existence-philosophy is the way of thought by means of which man seeks to become himself; it makes use of expert knowledge while at the same time going beyond it. This way of thought does not cognise objects, but elucidates and makes actual the being of the thinker. Brought into a state of suspense by having transcended the cognitions of the world (as the adoption of a philosophical attitude towards the world) that fixate being, it appeals to its own freedom (as the elucidation of existence) and gains space for its own unconditioned activity through conjuring up Transcendence (as metaphysics).

. . . Existence-philosophy cannot discover any solution, but can only become real in the multiplicity of thought proceeding from extant origins in the communication from one to another. . . . It awakens what it does not itself know; it elucidates and gives impetus, but it does not fixate. . . . Existence-philosophy may lapse into pure subjectivity. Then selfhood is misunderstood as the being of the ego, which solipsistically circumscribes itself as life that wishes to be nothing more. But genuine existence-philosophy is that appealing questioning in which, today, man is again seeking to come to his true self. Obviously, therefore, it is only found where people wrestle on its behalf. Out of a chance-medley with sociological, psychological, and anthropological thought, it may degenerate into a sophistical masquerade. Now censured as individualism, now used as a justification for personal shamelessness, it becomes the perilous foundation of a hysterical philosophy. But where it remains genuine, where it remains true to itself, it is uniquely effective in promoting all that makes man genuinely human.

The elucidation of existence, being directed at no object, leads to no result. A clarification of consciousness stimulates claims but does not bring fulfillment. As cognitive beings, we have to resign ourselves to it. For I am not what I cognise, nor do I cognise what I am. Instead of cognising my existence, I can only inaugurate the process of clarification. . . .

Reason and Existenz

Reason is not quite the substance out of which philosophy arises. For philosophy must ground itself in potential Existenz, which, for its part, can only unfold in rationality. I am that which is capable of reason but which is not made up of pure reason. If reason is not substantial, it is also true that nothing else is substantial without reason as its condition.

I can speak of Reason, personify it, and pay my respects to it as the condition of all truth for me. But it is never a permanent thing; rather it constitutes a continuous task in time. It is not an end in itself; but rather a medium. It is that through which everything else preserves its nature, is clarified, corroborated, and recognized. It is as though without reason everything were asleep like a seed.

I can produce nothing by reason alone. I must always encounter in it that other through which it itself is. This can be shown in every action of reason. Nothing real can be merely excogitated; and therefore Transcendence, for example, cannot be proven. But the pure thinking of reason which is not valid as the determinate knowledge of anything (which determinate knowledge always depends upon something else through its intuition or its mere givenness)—such reason is itself an act of Existenz in a particular form. Existenz in a self-positing cognition of its own Transcendence is a thinking which as such is an experience of its own being; that which is unavoidably connected with the consciousness of my Existenz is not thereby proven for the understanding as such, but exists for this Existenz which is clarifying itself validly in reason. . . . It is the nature of reason to be uncreative in itself, and precisely for this cause it can be universal, and through its universality it can bring the creative everywhere into act. There is nothing which can withdraw itself from contact with reason, and nothing which does not authentically emerge for the first time through either the positive or negative conditions of reason. . . . For there lies in rationality, when it is grasped in its radicality, multidimensionality, and in its connection with Existenz, a trust in itself, as though it must always still be possible. How far it actually succeeds however is a matter of experience. . . . But even if it finally found no echo in all the world, it still could not despair in itself. For it alone can see both itself and its alternatives, can clarify the ultimate shipwreck and the absolutely irrational in their rationality, and thereby first let them emerge into being.

"Existenz" is the concreteness of life, in which a self wills its own authenticity and reaches toward possibility; but without reason it would dissolve into mere sensation, into impulse, and at length into violence. Reason works in understanding, in the longing for order, and in the drive toward being in its fullness. Man does not, however, commence his life as a reflective being or a "rational animal," any more than he comes into it as an existing individual. At first, he simply exists, a primitive and non-reflective consciousness. He is in-the-world, "intentionally" related to it through his moods, attachments, childish "care" and concern. He is a Dasein, as Heidegger says; but, if he is to be a reflective creature—more than a lived body—he must launch himself into the future by breaking from mere "thereness." In disruption, in unease, he must begin to become.

MARTIN HEIDEGGER

What Is Philosophy?

Astonishment, as *pathos,* is the . . . beginning of philosophy. We must understand the Greek word *arche* (beginning) in its fullest sense. It names that from which something proceeds. But this "from where" is not left behind in the process of going out, but the beginning rather becomes that which . . . governs. The *pathos* of astonishment thus does not simply stand at the beginning of philosophy. . . . Astonishment carries and pervades philosophy. . . . We usually translate *pathos* with passion, ebullition of emotion. But *pathos* is connected with *paschein,* to suffer, endure, undergo, to be borne along by. . . . Only if we understand *pathos* as being attuned to, can we also characterize *thaumazein,* astonishment, more exactly . . . We step back, as it were, from being, from the fact that it is as it is and not otherwise. . . .

What Is Metaphysics?

Only because Nothing is revealed in the very basis of our *Da-sein* is it possible for the utter strangeness of what-is to dawn on us. Only when the strangeness of what-is forces itself upon us does it awaken and invite our wonder. Only because of wonder, that is to say, the revelation of Nothing, does the "Why?" spring to our lips. Only because this "Why?" is possible as such can we seek for reasons and proofs in a definite way. Only because we can ask and prove are we fated to become enquirers in this life.

The enquiry into Nothing puts us, the enquirers, in question. It is a metaphysical one.

Man's *Da-sein* can only relate to what-is by projecting into Nothing. Going beyond what-is is of the essence of *Da-sein.* But this "going beyond" is metaphysics itself.

. . . Because the truth of metaphysics is so unfathomable there is always the lurking danger of profoundest error. Hence no scientific discipline can hope to equal the seriousness of metaphysics. . . .

Philosophy is only set in motion by leaping with all its being, as only it can, into the ground-possibilities of being as a whole. For this leap the following things are of crucial importance: firstly, leaving room for what-is-in-totality; secondly, letting oneself go into Nothing, that is to say, freeing oneself from the idols we all have and to which we are wont to go cringing; lastly, letting this "suspense" range where it will, so that it may continually swing back again to the ground-question of metaphysics. . . .

Readiness for dread is to say "Yes!" to the inwardness of things, to fulfil the highest demand which alone touches man to the quick. Man alone of all beings, when addressed by the voice of Being, experiences the marvel of all marvels, that what-is *is*. Therefore the being that is called in its very essence to the truth of Being is always attuned in an essential sense. The clear courage for essential dread guarantees that most mysterious of all possibilities: the experience of Being. . . . To the degree that we degrade this essential dread and the relationship cleared within it for Man to Being, we demean the essence of courage. Courage can endure Nothing: it knows, in the abyss of terror, the all but untrodden region of Being, that "clearing" where everything that "is" returns into *what* it is and is able to be. . . . But Being is not a product of thinking. It is more likely that essential thinking is an occurrence of Being.

For this reason the scarcely formulated question now forces itself on us as to whether this kind of thinking conforms to the law of its truth when it only follows the thinking whose forms and rules constitute "logic." Why (ought) we to put this word in inverted commas? In order to indicate that "logic" is only *one* exposition of the nature of thinking, and one which, as its name shows, is based on the experience of Being as attained in Greek thought. The animus against "logic"—the logical degeneration of which can be seen in "logistics"—derives from the knowledge of that thinking which has its source not in the observation of the objectivity of what-is, but in the experience of the truth of Being. "Exact" thinking is never the strictest thinking, if the essence of strictness lies in the strenuousness with which knowledge keeps in touch with the essential feature of what-is. "Exact" thinking merely binds itself to the calculation of what-is and ministers to this alone. . . .

It remains important to calculate, to keep in touch with the world in which each individual is cast. Each one must make his world intelligible by acting upon it, using it, inquiring into it in diverse ways, structuring it by means of language. If he has the courage to attune himself inwardly, however, to confront Nothing, to live in astonishment and suspense, he will—by means of learning and thinking—transcend what was first disclosed to him through his own bodily involvements, through the spectrum of his moods, even through calculation. He will begin to "signify," to symbolize more and more diversely what was once merely sensed and perceived; he will begin to be.

MAURICE MERLEAU-PONTY

The Primacy of Perception

We grasp external space through our bodily situation. A "corporeal or postural schema" gives us at every moment a global, practical, and implicit notion of the relation between our body and things, of our hold on them. A system of possible movements, or "motor projects," radiates from us to our environment. Our body is not in space like things; it inhabits or haunts space. It

applies itself to space like a hand to an instrument, and
when we wish to move about we do not move the body
as we move an object. We transport it without instruments as if by magic, since it is ours and because through
it we have direct access to space. For us the body is much
more than an instrument or a means; it is our expression
to the world, the visible form of our intentions. Even
our most secret affective movements, those most deeply
tied to the humoral infrastructure, help to shape our
perception of things.

Now if perception is thus the common act of all our
motor and affective functions, no less than the sensory,
we must rediscover the structure of the perceived world
through a process similar to that of an archaeologist. For
the structure of the perceived world is buried under the
sedimentations of later knowledge. Digging down to the
perceived world, we see that sensory qualities are not
opaque, indivisible "givens," which are simply exhibited
to a remote consciousness—a favorite idea of classical
philosophy. We see too that colors . . . are themselves
different modalities of our co-existence with the world.
We also find that spatial forms or distances are not so
much relations between different points in objective
space as they are relations between these points and a
central perspective—our body. In short, these relations
are different ways for external stimuli to test, to solicit,
and to vary our grasp on the world, our horizontal and
vertical anchorage in a place and in a here-and-now.
We find that perceived things, unlike geometrical objects, are not bounded entities whose laws of construction
we possess *a priori,* but that they are open, inexhaustible
systems which we recognize through a certain style of
development, although we are never able, in principle,
to explore them entirely, and even though they never
give us more than profiles and perspectival views of
themselves. Finally, we find that the perceived world, in
its turn, is not a pure object of thought without fissures
or lacunae; it is, rather, like a universal style shared in
by all perceptual beings, we can never presume that its

work is finished. Our world, as Malebranche said, is an "unfinished task."

If we now wish to characterize a subject capable of this perceptual experience, it obviously will not be a self-transparent thought, absolutely present to itself without the interference of its body and its history. The perceiving subject is not this absolute thinker; rather, it functions according to a natal pact between our body and the world, between ourselves and our body. Given a perpetually new natural and historical situation to control, the perceiving subject undergoes a continued birth; at each instant it is something new. Every incarnate subject is like an open notebook in which we do not yet know what will be written. Or it is like a new language; we do not know what works it will accomplish but only that, once it has appeared, it cannot fail to say little or much, to have a history and a meaning. The very productivity or freedom of human life, far from denying our situation, utilizes it and turns it into a means of expression.

. . . It seems to me that knowledge and the communication with others which it presupposes not only are original formations with respect to the perceptual life but also they preserve and continue our perceptual life even while transforming it. Knowledge and communication sublimate rather than suppress our incarnation, and the characteristic operation of the mind is in the movement by which we recapture our corporeal existence and use it to symbolize instead of merely to co-exist. Through its "sensory fields" and its whole organization the body is, so to speak, predestined to model itself on the natural aspects of the world. But as an active body capable of gestures, of expression, and finally of language, it turns back on the world to signify it.

The situation in which learning (speaking, thinking) must begin is not one in which an individual finds himself in an already "given" natural world, determinate or indeterminate. It must be granted that there exists such a world, and there exists a natural creature (an "empirical ego") within it, along with other human beings and the various properties of everyday life. But existential awareness demands a breaking off from that namable and familiar context. It demands a focusing upon the world as revealed by the consciousness engaged in intentional activity within a concrete, lived situation. At the beginning this consciousness is non-reflective; the world as revealed is inchoate; horizons and boundaries are vague; "meaning" is not yet.

FRANZ KAFKA

Amerika

A narrow outside balcony ran along the whole length of Karl's room. But what would have been at home the highest vantage point in the town allowed him here little more than a view of one street, which ran perfectly straight between two rows of squarely chopped buildings and therefore seemed to be fleeing into the distance, where the outlines of a cathedral loomed enormous in a dense haze. From morning to evening and far into the dreaming night that street was the channel for a constant stream of traffic which, seen from above, looked like an inextricable confusion, for ever newly improvised, of fore-shortened human figures and the roofs of all kinds of vehicles, sending into the upper air another confusion, more riotous and complicated, of noises, dust, and smells, all of it enveloped and penetrated by a flood of light which the multitudinous objects in the street scattered, carried off and again busily brought back, with an effect as palpable to the dazzled eye as if a glassroof stretched over the street were being violently smashed into fragments at every moment.

This is one way to image the world as immediately experienced, not yet understood. It is one way of breaking with—or "bracketing"—the world as conceptualized. Another is to regain the original mode of appropriating the environment, the corporeal and intentional consciousness of situation. Not only does this return—or rediscovery—render experience suddenly strange and problematic; it provides an opportunity for understanding the formlessness of the precognitive state, the suggestive concreteness in which apprehension of being begins to stir.

JEAN-PAUL SARTRE

Nausea

The thing which was waiting was on the alert, it has pounced on me, it flows through me, I am filled with it. It's nothing: I am the Thing. Existence, liberated, detached, floods over me. I exist.

I exist. It's sweet, so sweet, so slow. And light; you'd think it floated all by itself. It stirs. It brushes by me, melts and vanishes. Gently, gently. There is bubbling water in my mouth. I swallow. It slides down my throat, it caresses me—and now it comes up again into my mouth. For ever I shall have a little pool of whitish water in my mouth—lying low—grazing my tongue. And this pool is still me. And the tongue. And the throat is me.

I see my hand spread out on the table. It lives—it is me. It opens, the fingers open and point. It is lying on its back. It shows me its fat belly. It looks like an animal turned upside down. The fingers are the paws. I amuse myself by moving them very rapidly, like the claws of a crab which has fallen on its back.

The crab is dead; the claws draw up and close over the belly of my hand. I see the nails—the only part of me that doesn't live. And once more. My hand turns

over, spreads out flat on its stomach, offers me the sight
of its back. A silvery back, shining a little—like a fish
except for the red hairs on the knuckles. I feel my hand.
I am these two beasts struggling at the end of my arms.
My hand scratches one of its paws with the nail of the
other paw; I feel its weight on the table which is not
me. It's long, long, this impression of weight, it doesn't
pass. There is no reason for it to pass. It becomes intolerable . . . I draw back my hand and put it in my
pocket; but immediately I feel the warmth of my thigh
through the stuff. I pull my hand out of my pocket and
let it hang against the back of the chair. Now I feel a
weight at the end of my arm. It pulls a little, softly, in-
sinuatingly it exists. I don't insist: no matter where I put
it it will go on existing; I can't suppress it, nor can I suppress the rest of my body, the sweaty warmth which soils
my shirt, nor all this warm obesity which turns lazily, as
if someone were stirring it with a spoon, nor all the sensations going on inside, going, coming, mounting from
my side to my armpit or quietly vegetating from morning
to night, in their usual corner.

I jump up: it would be much better if I could only
stop thinking. Thoughts are the dullest things. Duller
than flesh. They stretch out and there's no end to them
and they leave a funny taste in the mouth. Then there
are words, inside the thoughts, unfinished words, a
sketchy sentence which constantly returns: "I have to
fi . . . I ex . . . Dead . . . M. De Roll is dead . . . I
am not . . . I ex . . ." It goes, it goes, . . . and there's
no end to it. It's worse than the rest because I feel
responsible and have complicity in it. For example, this
sort of painful rumination: I *exist*, I am the one who
keeps it up. I. The body lives by itself once it has begun.
But thought—*I* am the one who continues it, unrolls it.
I exist. How serpentine is this feeling of existing—I un-
wind it, slowly. . . . If I could keep myself from thinking! I try, and succeed: my head seems to fill with
smoke . . . and then it starts again: "Smoke . . . not
to think . . . don't want to think . . . I think I don't

want to think. I mustn't think that I don't want to think. Because that's still a thought." Will there never be an end to it?

Being and Nothingness

. . . The immediate consciousness which I have of perceiving does not permit me either to judge or to will or to be ashamed. It does not know my perception, does not posit it; all that there is of intention in my actual consciousness is directed toward the outside, toward the world. In turn, this spontaneous consciousness of my perception is constitutive of my perceptive consciousness. In other words, every positional consciousness of an object is at the same time a non-positional consciousness of itself. If I count the cigarettes which are in that case, I have the impression of disclosing an objective property of this collection of cigarettes: they are a dozen. This property appears to my consciousness as a property existing in the world. It is very possible that I have no positional consciousness of counting them. Then I do not know myself as counting. Proof of this is that children who are capable of making an addition spontaneously cannot *explain* subsequently how they set about it. Piaget's tests, which show this, constitute an excellent refutation of the formula . . . [that] to know is to know that one knows. . . . Thus reflection has no kind of primacy over the consciousness reflected-on. It is not reflection which reveals the consciousness reflected-on to itself. Quite the contrary, it is the non-reflective consciousness which renders the reflection possible; there is a pre-reflective cogito which is the condition of the Cartesian cogito.

Being may be revealed to the pre-reflective consciousness as sticky and slimy, continually sucking the striving human being back into his own past and into mere sensation. Reaching out toward completeness and reflective-

ness, every child in the process of becoming must fight against being absorbed into the "gluey, the sticky, the hazy. . . ." His very learning involves a struggle against inertia, resistance to the blank contemplation of brute fact.

Being and Nothingness

. . . the slimy offers a horrible image; it is horrible in itself for a consciousness to become *slimy*. This is because the being of the slimy is a soft clinging, there is a sly solidarity and complicity in all its leechlike parts, a vague, soft effort made by each to individualize itself, followed by a falling back and flattening out that is emptied of the individual, sucked in on all sides by the substance. A consciousness which became slimy would be transformed by the thick stickiness of its ideas. From the time of our upsurge into the world, we are haunted by the image of a consciousness which would like to launch forth into the future, toward a projection of self, and which at the very moment when it was conscious of arriving there would be slyly held back by the invisible suction of the past and which would have to assist in its own slow dissolution in this past which it was fleeing, would have to aid in the invasion of its project by a thousand parasites until finally it completely lost itself. . . . The horror of the slimy is the horrible fear that time might become slimy, that facticity might progress continually and insensibly and absorb the For-itself which *exists it*. It is the fear not of death, not of the pure In-itself, not of nothingness, but of a particular type of being, which does not actually exist any more than the In-itself For-itself and which is only *represented* by the slimy. It is an ideal being which I reject with all my strength. . . . Henceforth for the For-itself there appears a new danger, a threatening mode of being which must be avoided, a concrete category which it will discover everywhere. The slimy does not symbolize any psychic attitude *a priori;* it manifests a certain relation of being with itself and this relation has originally a psychic quality because I have discovered in it a plan of appropriation and because the sliminess has returned my image to me. Thus I am enriched from my first contact with the slimy, by a valid ontological pattern beyond the distinction between psychic and non-psychic, which will interpret the meaning of being and of all the existents of a certain category, this category arising, moreover, like an empty skeletal framework before the experience with different kinds of sliminess. I have projected it into the world by my original project when faced with the slimy; it is an objective structure of the world and at the same time an antivalue; that is, it determines an area where slimy objects will arrange themselves. Henceforth each time that an object will manifest to me this relation of being, whether it is a matter of a handshake, of a smile, or of a thought, it will be apprehended by definition as slimy; that is, beyond its phenomenological context, it will appear to me as constituting along with pitch, glue, honey, etc. the great ontological region of sliminess.

The world, therefore, reveals itself to the young child in various immediate ways; and the child appropriates the world accordingly, never entirely forgetting what was originally disclosed. Even as he projects himself forward, he carries with him an awareness of brute existence—of "senselessness"—which all the arrangements of social life are devised to obscure. But there is in the perception of meaninglessness (or of "facticity") a potential opportunity to impose meaning, if only by contemplating or ordering the past, or by telling "stories" about existing in the present.

Nausea

This is what I thought: for the most banal event to become an adventure, you must (and this is enough) begin to recount it. This is what fools people: a man is always a teller of tales, he lives surrounded by his stories and the stories of others, he sees everything that happens to him through them; and he tries to live his own life as if he were telling a story.

But you have to choose: live or tell. For example, when I was in Hamburg, with that Erna girl I didn't trust and who was afraid of me, I led a funny sort of life. But I was in the middle of it, I didn't think about it. And then one evening, in a little cafe in San Pauli, she left me to go to the ladies' room. I stayed alone, there was a phonograph playing "Blue Skies." I began to tell myself what had happened since I landed. I told myself, "The third evening, as I was going into a dance hall called *La Grotte Bleue,* I noticed a large woman, half seas over. And that woman is the one I am waiting for now, listening to 'Blue Skies,' the woman who is going to come back and sit down at my right and put her arms around my neck." Then I felt violently that I was having an adventure. But Erna came back and sat down beside me, she wound her arms around my neck and I hated her without knowing why. I understand now: one had to begin living again and the adventure was fading out.

Nothing happens while you live. The scenery changes, people come in and go out, that's all. There are no beginnings. Days are tacked on to days without rhyme or reason, an interminable, monotonous addition. From time to time you make a semi-total: you say: I've been travelling for three years, I've been in Bouville for three years. Neither is there any end: you never leave a woman, a friend, a city in one go. And then everything looks alike: Shanghai, Moscow, Algiers, everything is the same after two weeks. There are moments—rarely—when you make a landmark, you realize that you're going with a woman, in some messy business. The time of a flash. After that, the procession starts again, you begin to add up hours and days: Monday, Tuesday, Wednesday. April, May, June. 1924, 1925, 1926.

That's living. But everything changes when you tell about it; it's a change no one notices; the proof is that people talk about true stories. As if there could possibly be true stories; things happen one way and we tell about them in the opposite sense. You seem to start at the beginning: "It was a fine autumn evening in 1922. I was a notary's clerk in Marommes." And in reality you have started at the end. It was there, invisible and present, it is the one which gives to words the pomp and value of a beginning. "I was out walking, I had left the town without realizing it, I was thinking about my money troubles." This sentence, taken simply for what it is, means that the man was absorbed, morose, a hundred leagues from an adventure, exactly in the mood to let things happen without noticing them. But the end is there, transforming everything. For us, the man is already the hero of the story. His moroseness, his money troubles are much more precious than ours, they are all gilded by the light of future passions. And the story goes on in the reverse; instants have stopped piling themselves in a lighthearted way one on top of the other, they are snapped up by the end of the story which draws them and each one of them in turn, draws out the preceding instant: "It was night, the street was deserted." The phrase is cast out negligently, it seems superfluous; but we do not let ourselves be caught and we put it aside: this is a piece of information whose value we shall subsequently appreciate. And we feel that the hero has lived all the details of this night like annunciations, promises, or even that he lived only those that were promises, blind and deaf to all that did not herald adventure. We forget that the future was not yet there; the man was walking in a night without forethought, a night which offered him a choice of dull rich prizes, and he did not make his choice.

I wanted the moments of my life to follow and order themselves like those of a life remembered. You might as well try and catch time by the tail.

To tell about it, to put it into symbolic terms, is to impose a pattern on the inherently formless. It is, in re-

sponse to the human longing for order and "sense," to break with the denseness and flux of the immediately experienced, to "transcend" the pre-reflective, to make reason one with "existenz." And thus it is exemplary. It leads to the many modes of organizing experience by means of concepts; it indicates the existential significance of the ability to categorize, to pattern, to think. A rebellion which is meaningfulness becomes possible: a rebellion launched by the consciousness that "I exist" and by the experience of the "absurd."

ALBERT CAMUS

The Myth of Sisyphus

All great deeds and all great thoughts have a ridiculous beginning. Great works are often born on a street-corner or in a restaurant's revolving door. So it is with absurdity. The absurd world more than others derives its nobility from that abject birth. In certain situations, replying "nothing" when asked what one is thinking about may be pretense in a man. Those who are loved are well aware of this. But if that reply is sincere, if it symbolizes that odd state of soul in which the void becomes eloquent, in which the chain of daily gestures is broken, in which the heart vainly seeks the link that will connect it again, then it is as it were the first sign of absurdity.

It happens that the stage sets collapse. Rising, street-car, four hours in the office or the factory, meal, streetcar, four hours of work, meal, sleep, and Monday Tuesday Wednesday Thursday Friday and Saturday according to the same rhythm—this path is easily followed most of the time. But one day the "why" arises and everything begins in that weariness tinged with amazement. "Begins"— that is important. Weariness comes at the end of the acts of a mechanical life, but at the same time it inaugurates the impulse of consciousness. It awakens consciousness and provokes what follows. What follows is the gradual return into the chain or it is the definitive awakening. At the end of the awakening comes, in time, the consequence: suicide or recovery. In itself weariness has something sickening about it. Here, I must conclude it is good. For everything begins with consciousness and nothing is worth anything except through it. There is nothing original about these remarks. But they are obvious; that is enough for a while. . . . Mere "anxiety," as Heidegger says, is at the source of everything.

Likewise and during every day of an unillustrious life, time carries us. But a moment always comes when we have to carry it. We live on the future: "tomorrow," "later on," "when you have made your way," "you will understand when you are old enough." Such irrelevancies are wonderful, for, after all, it's a matter of dying. Yet a day comes when a man notices or says that he is thirty. Thus he asserts his youth. But simultaneously he situates himself in relation to time. He takes his place in it. He admits that he stands at a certain point on a curve that he acknowledges having to travel to its end. He belongs to time, and by the horror that seizes him, he recognizes his worst enemy. Tomorrow, he was longing for tomorrow, whereas everything in him ought to reject it. . . .

A step lower and strangeness creeps in: perceiving that the world is "dense," sensing to what a degree a stone is foreign and irreducible to us, with what intensity nature or a landscape can negate us. At the heart of all beauty lies something inhuman, and these hills, the softness of the sky, the outline of these trees at this very minute lose the illusory meaning with which we had clothed them. . . . The primitive hostility of the world rises up to face us across milennia. For a second we cease to understand it because for centuries we have understood in it solely the images and designs that we had attributed to it beforehand, because henceforth we lack the power to make use of that artifice. . . .

Men, too, secrete the inhuman. At certain moments of lucidity, the mechanical aspect of their gestures, their meaningless pantomime makes silly everything that surrounds them. A man is talking on the telephone behind a glass partition; you cannot hear him, but you see his incomprehensible dumb show: you wonder why he is alive. This discomfort in the face of man's own inhumanity, this incalculable tumble before the image of what we are, this "nausea," as a writer of today calls it, is also the absurd. . . .

The mind's first step is to distinguish what is true from what is false. However, as soon as thought reflects on itself, what it first discovers is a contradiction. . . . no one has furnished a clearer and more elegant demonstration of the business than Aristotle: "The often ridiculed consequence of these opinions is that they destroy themselves. For by asserting that all is true we assert the truth of the contrary assertion and consequently the falsity of our own thesis." . . . This vicious circle is but the first of a series in which the mind that studies itself gets lost in a giddy whirling. . . . Whatever may be the plays on words, and the acrobatics of logic, to understand is, above all, to unify. The mind's deepest desire, even in its most elaborate operations, parallels man's unconscious feeling in the face of his universe: it is an insistence upon familiarity, an appetite for clarity. . . . That nostalgia for unity, that appetite for the absolute illustrates the essential impulse of the human drama. But the fact of that nostalgia's existence does not imply that it is to be immediately satisfied. . . .

And here are trees and I know their gnarled surface, water and I feel its taste. These scents of grass and stars at night, certain evenings when the heart relaxes—how shall I negate this world whose power and strength I feel? Yet all the knowledge on earth will give me nothing to assure me that this world is mine. You describe it to me and you teach me to classify it. You enumerate its laws and in my thirst for knowledge I admit that they are true. You take apart its mechanism and my hope increases. At the final stage you teach me that this wondrous multicolored universe can be reduced to the atom and that the atom can be reduced to the electron. All this is good and I wait for you to continue. But you tell me of an invisible planetary system in which electrons gravitate around a nucleus. You explain this world to me with an image. I realize then that you have been reduced to poetry: I shall never know. Have I the time to become indignant? You have already changed theories. So that science that was to teach me everything ends up in a hypothesis, that lucidity founders in metaphor, that uncertainty is resolved in a work of art. What need had I of so many efforts? The soft lines of these hills and the hand of evening on this troubled heart teach me much more. I have returned to my beginning. I realize that if through science I can seize phenomena and enumerate them, I cannot, for all that, apprehend the world. Were I to trace its entire relief with my finger, I should not know any more. And you give the choice between a description that is sure but that teaches me nothing and hypotheses that claim to teach me but that are not sure. A stranger to myself and to the world, armed solely with a thought that negates itself as soon as it asserts, what is this condition in which I can have peace only by refusing to know and to live, in which the appetite for conquest bumps into walls that defy its assaults? To will is to stir up paradoxes. Everything is ordered in such a way as to bring into being that poisoned peace produced by thoughtlessness, lack of heart, or fatal renunciations.

Hence the intelligence, too, tells me in its own way that this world is absurd. Its contrary, blind reason, may well claim that all is clear; I was waiting for proof and longing for it to be right. But despite so many pretentious centuries and over the heads of so many eloquent and persuasive men, I know that is false. . . . That universal reason, practical or ethical, that determinism, those categories that explain everything are enough to make a decent man laugh. They have nothing to do with the mind. They negate its profound truth, which is to be enchained. In this unintelligible and limited universe, man's fate henceforth assumes its meaning. . . . The world in itself is not reasonable, that is all that can be said. But what is absurd is the confrontation of this irrational and the wild longing for clarity whose call echoes in the human heart. The absurd depends as much on man as on the world. For the moment it is all that links them together. . . . If I hold to be true that absurdity determines my relationship with life, if I become thoroughly imbued with that sentiment that seizes me in the face of the world's scenes, with that lucidity imposed on me by the pursuit of a science, I must sacrifice everything to these certainties and I must see them squarely to be able to maintain them. Above all, I must adapt my behavior to them and pursue them in all their consequences. I am speaking here of decency. But I want to know beforehand if thought can live in those deserts.

Decency is to keep thought alive in response to the awareness of the problematic, which is the desert, which is the absurd. Rebellion on behalf of decency is rebellion in the name of created orders, exemplified by art.

The Rebel

The contradiction is this: man rejects the world as it is, without accepting the necessity of escaping it. In fact, men cling to the world and by far the greatest majority do not want to abandon it. Far from always wanting to forget it, they suffer . . . . from not being able to possess it completely enough. . . . Except for vivid moments of fulfillment, all reality for them is incomplete. . . . There is not one human being who, above a certain elementary level of consciousness, does not exhaust himself in trying to find formulae or attitudes which will give his existence the unity it lacks. Appearance and action, the dandy and the revolutionary, all demand unity, in order to exist and in order to exist on this earth. . . . It is therefore justifiable to say that man has an idea of a better world than this. But better does not mean different, it means unified. This passion which lifts the mind above the common-places of a dispersed world, from which it nevertheless detaches itself, is the passion for unity. . . . Religion or crime, every human endeavour, in fact, finally obeys this unreasonable desire and claims to give life a form it does not have. The same impulse, which can lead to the adoration of the heavens or the destruction of man, also leads to creative literature which derives its serious content at this source.

What, in fact, is a novel but a universe in which action is endowed with form, where final words are pronounced, where people possess one another completely and where life assumes the aspects of destiny? The world of the novel is only a rectification of the world we live in, in pursuance of man's deepest wishes. . . . Here we have an imaginary world, therefore, which is created from the rectification of the actual world—a world where suffering can, if it wishes, continue until death, where passions are never distracted, where people are prey to obsessions and are always present to each other. Man is finally able to give himself the alleviating form and limits which he pursues in vain in his own life.

If persons are not to be understood in terms of some common "essence" or in the light of some abstraction like "humanity" or "man," they must be viewed as existent beings involved in creating themselves. And since nothing external can give continuity to his existence, each single person must give himself reality by making critical choices in all the situations of his life, committing himself to what he chooses, and renewing himself by making further choices—in his freedom, without guidance or guarantee. This is the way he comes to be a full person, an identity. It is the way he authenticates himself as an individual. Education, therefore, must provide opportunities for him to make the decisions which give him continuity as an existing individual. The skills, the subject matters which are taught, must be presented as possibilities which each individual can appropriate for himself as he chooses himself, as he creates himself as a reflective being.

SOREN KIERKEGAARD

The Journals: 1847, 1854

People are not so completely depraved as really to desire evil, but they are blinded and do not really know what they are doing. Everything depends upon luring a decision from them. A child may be rebellious against his father in small things for a long time, but if once its father can drive it to a real revolt it is far nearer salvation.

HUMAN EDUCATION

Providence has given every man certain characteristics. The important thing in life should therefore be to develop that characteristic, strengthened and confirmed by the conflicts which it must produce with its surroundings.

Human education, on the other hand, is demoralizing, is calculated to teach a man how not to have an air, how not to use a word, not to undertake the least thing without having a guarantee that numbers of others have done the same thing before him. . . .

The Point of View

That if real success is to attend the effort to bring a man to a definite position, one must first of all take pains to find HIM where he is and begin there.

This is the secret of the art of helping others. Anyone who has not mastered this is himself deluded when he proposes to help others. In order to help another effectively, I must understand more than he—yet first of all surely I must understand what he understands. If I do not know that, my greater understanding will be of no help to him. If, however, I am disposed to plume myself on my greater understanding, it is because I am vain or proud, so that at bottom, instead of benefiting him, I want to be admired. But all true effort to help begins with self-humiliation: the helper must first humble himself under him he would help, and therewith must understand that to help does not mean to be a sovereign but to be a servant, that to help does not mean to be ambitious but to be patient, that to help means to endure for the time being the imputation that one is in the wrong and does not understand what the other understands. . . . For to be a teacher does not mean simply to affirm that such a thing is so, or to deliver a lecture, etc. No, to be a teacher in the right sense is to be a learner. Instruction begins when you, the teacher, learn from the learner, put yourself in his place so that you may understand what he understands and in the way he understands it. . . .

The teacher's obligation is to be patient enough to permit deliberation and decision by each of those he is trying to help. If his students do not choose, each in the light of his own contingent existence and his own limitations, they will not become ethical beings; if they are not ethical beings—in search of their own ethical reality— they are not individuals; if they are not individuals, they will not learn.

Either / Or

. . . The choice itself is decisive for the content of personality, through the choice the personality immerses itself in the thing chosen, and when it does not choose it withers away in consumption. For an instant it is as if, for an instant it may seem as if the thing with regard to which a choice was made lay outside the chooser, that he stands in no relationship to it, that he can preserve a state of indifference over against it. This is the instant of deliberation, but this, like the Platonic instant, has no existence, least of all in the abstract sense in which you would hold it fast, and the longer one stares at it the less it exists. That which has to be chosen stands in the deepest relationship to the chooser and, when it is a question of a choice involving a life problem, the individual must naturally be living in the meantime; hence it comes about that the longer he postpones the choice the easier it is for him to alter its character, notwithstanding that he is constantly deliberating and deliberating, and believes that thereby he is holding the alternatives distinctly apart. When life's either/or is regarded in this way, one is not easily tempted to jest with it. One sees, then, that the inner drift of the personality leaves no time for thought-experiments, that it constantly hastens onward and in one way or another posits this alternative or that, making the choice more difficult the next instant, because what has thus been posited must be revoked. Think of the captain on his ship at the instant when it has to come about. He will perhaps be able to say, "I can either do this or that"; but unless he is a pretty poor navigator, he will be aware at the same time that the ship is all the while making its usual headway, and that therefore it is only an instant when it is indifferent whether he does this or that. So it is with a man. If he forgets to take account of the headway, there comes at last an instant when there no longer is any question of an either/or, not because he has chosen but because he has neglected to choose, which is equivalent to saying, because others have chosen for him, because he has lost himself.

. . . the instant of choice is very serious, not so much on account of the rigorous cogitation involved in weighing the alternatives, not on account of the multiplicity of thoughts which attach themselves to every link in the chain, but rather because there is danger afoot, danger that the next instant it may not be equally in my power to choose, that something already has been lived which must be lived over again. To think that for an instant one can keep one's personality a blank, or that strictly speaking one can break off and bring to a halt the course of personal life, is a delusion. The personality is already interested in the choice before one chooses, and when the choice is postponed the personality chooses unconsciously, or the choice is made by obscure powers within it. So when at last the choice is made, one discovers . . . that there is something which must be done over again, something which must be revoked, and this is often very difficult.

Therefore it is important to choose and to choose in time.

. . . but an aesthetic choice is no choice. The act of

choosing is essentially a proper and stringent expression
of the ethical. Whenever in a stricter sense there is a
question of either/or, one can always be sure that the
ethical is involved. The only absolute either/or is the
choice between good and evil, but that is also absolutely
ethical. The aesthetic choice is entirely immediate, or it
loses itself in the multifarious. Thus when a young girl
follows the choice of her heart, this choice, however
beautiful it may be, is in the strictest sense no choice,
since it is entirely immediate. When a man deliberates
aesthetically upon a multitude of life's problems . . . he
does not easily get one either/or but a whole multiplicity,
because the determining factor in the choice is not accentuated, and because when one does not choose absolutely one chooses only for the moment, and therefore
can choose something different the next moment. The
ethical choice is therefore in a certain sense much easier,
much simpler, but in another sense it is infinitely harder.
He who would define his life task ethically has ordinarily
not so considerable a selection to choose from; on the
other hand, the act of choice has far more importance for
him. . . . I should like to say that in making a choice
it is not so much a question of choosing the right as of
the energy, the consciousness, the pathos with which one
chooses. Thereby the personality announces its inner infinity, and thereby, in turn, the personality is consoli-
dated. Therefore, even if a man were to choose the
wrong, he will nevertheless discover, precisely by reason
of the energy with which he chose, that he has chosen
the wrong. For, the choice being made with the whole inwardness of his personality, his nature is purified and he
himself brought into immediate relation to the eternal
Power whose omnipresence interpenetrates the whole of
existence. . . .

   What is it, then, that I distinguish in my either/or?
Is it good and evil? No, I would only bring you up to
the point where the choice between the evil and the good
acquires significance for you. Everything hinges on
this. . . .

My either/or does not in the first instance denote the choice between good and evil, it denotes the choice whereby one chooses good and evil/ or excludes them. Here the question is under what determinants one would contemplate the whole of existence and would himself live. That the man who chooses good and evil chooses the good is indeed true, but this becomes evident only afterwards; for the aesthetical is not the evil but neutrality, and that is the reason why I affirmed that it is the ethical which constitutes the choice. It is, therefore, not so much a question of choosing between willing the good *or* the evil, as of choosing to *will,* but by this in turn the good and the evil are posited.

The individual child moves between limitation and possibility; but he will only act upon his project of becoming a self if he takes seriously the responsibility of decisiveness and self-determination. At once, he must develop a sense of his own limitations, his own "necessity," so that the self toward which he yearns does not become "an abstract possibility" which merely flounders "in the possible."

The Sickness Unto Death

Possibility then appears to the self even greater and greater, more and more things become possible, because nothing becomes actual. At last it is as if everything were possible—but this is precisely when the abyss has swallowed up the self. Every little possibility even would require some time to become actuality. But finally the time which should be available for actuality becomes shorter and shorter, everything becomes more and more instantaneous. Possibility becomes more and more intense—but only in the sense of possibility, not in the sense of actuality; for in the sense of actuality the meaning of intensity is that at least something of that which is possible becomes actual. At the instant something appears possible, and then a new possibility makes its

appearance, at last this phantasmagoria moves so rapidly
that it is as if everything were possible—and this is precisely the last moment, when the individual becomes for
himself a mirage.

What the self now lacks is surely reality—so one
would commonly say, as one says of a man that he has
become unreal. But upon closer inspection it is really
necessity that the man lacks. For it is not true, as the
philosophers explain, that necessity is a unity of possibility and necessity. Nor is it merely due to lack of
strength when the soul goes astray in possibility—at least
this is not to be understood as people commonly understand it. What really is lacking is the power to obey, to
submit to the necessary in oneself, to what may be called
one's limit. Therefore the misfortune does not consist in
the fact that such a self did not amount to anything in
the world; no, the misfortune is that the man did not
become aware of himself, aware that the self he is, is a
perfectly definite something, and so is the necessary. On
the contrary, he lost himself, owing to the fact that this
self was seen fantastically reflected in the possible. Even
in looking at one's *self* in a mirror it is requisite to know
oneself; for, if not, one does not behold one's *self* but
merely a man. But the mirror of possibility is not an
ordinary mirror, it must be used with the utmost precau-
tion. For of this mirror it is true in the highest sense that
it is a false mirror. That the self looks so and so in the
possibility of itself is only half truth; for in the possibility
of itself the self is still far from itself. . . . So the
question is how the necessity of the self determines it
more precisely. A case analogous to possibility is when
the child is invited to participate in some pleasure or
another: the child is at once willing, but now it is a
question whether the parents will permit it—and as with
parents, so it is with necessity. . . .

The self, then, is always in process, but in process be-
tween possibility and necessity—the dialectical synthesis

of which is freedom. Possibility refers to what is not yet: the unrealized capacities of the individual self. Necessity refers to what the self itself experiences as the qualities of its particular existential situation: the strange, threatening features known by means of boredom and dread; the multiple influences exerted by personal relationships and institutions; the choices already made; the unique "characteristics" with which the person has been endowed, and which are being continuously confirmed. Immersed in situation, the self therefore is a "perfectly definite something," to be treated with "care" by each person, to be taken into account by the teacher who needs to "find HIM where he is."

FYODOR DOSTOEVSKY

Notes from Underground

"Ha! ha! ha! But you know there is no such thing as choice in reality, say what you like," you will interpose with a chuckle. "Science has succeeded in so far analyzing man that we know already that choice and what is called freedom of will is nothing else than—"

Stay, gentlemen, I meant to begin with that myself. I confess, I was rather frightened. I was just going to say that the devil only knows what choice depends on, and that perhaps that was a very good thing, but I remembered the teaching of science . . . and pulled myself up. And here you have begun upon it. Indeed, if there really is some day discovered a formula for all our desires and caprices—that is, an explanation of what they depend on, by what laws they arise, how they develop, what they are aiming at in one case and in another and so on, that is, a real mathematical formula—then, most likely, man will at once cease to feel desire, indeed he will be certain to. For who would want to choose by rule? Besides, he will at once be transformed from a human being into an organ-stop or something of the sort; for what is a man without desires, without free will, and without choice, if not a stop in an organ? What do you think? Let us reckon the chances—can such a thing happen or not?

"H'm!" you decide. "Our choice is usually mistaken from a false view of our advantage. We sometimes choose absolute nonsense because in our foolishness we see in that nonsense the easiest means of attaining a supposed advantage. But when all that is explained and worked out on paper . . . then certainly so-called desires will no longer exist. For if a desire should come into conflict with reason we shall then reason and not desire, because it will be impossible retaining our reason to be *senseless* in our desires, and in that way knowingly act against reason and desire to injure ourselves. And as all choice and reasoning can be really calculated—because there will some day be discovered the laws of our so-called free will—so, joking apart, there may one day be a something like a table constructed of them, so that we really shall choose in accordance with it. If, for instance, some day they calculate and prove to me that I made a long nose at some one because I could not help making a long nose at him and that I had to do it in that particular way, what *freedom* is left me, especially if I am a learned man and have taken my degree somewhere? . . ."

The necessities—and the ability to explain them—must be granted; but human choice remains the mode of translating necessity into freedom. As in the case of James Joyce's Stephen Daedalus, the determinisms of one's personal history can be transcended so long as one becomes conscious of them, so long as one tries "to encounter for the millionth time the reality of experience." It is possible then for the individual to say, like Stephen Daedalus, "I will take the risk," and break free.

FRIEDRICH NIETZSCHE

Thus Spake Zarathustra (*Third Part*)

Man is hard to discover—hardest of all for himself: often the spirit lies about the soul. Thus the spirit of gravity orders it. He, however, has discovered himself who says, "This is *my* good and evil"; with that he has reduced to silence the mole and dwarf who say, "Good for all, evil for all."

Verily, I also do not like those who consider everything good and this world the best. Such men I call the omni-satisfied. Omni-satisfaction, which knows how to taste everything, that is not the best taste. I honor the recalcitrant choosy tongues and stomachs, which have learned to say "I" and "yes" and "no." But to chew and digest everything—that is truly the swine's manner. Always to bray Yea-Yuh—that only the ass has learned, and whoever is of his spirit.

Deep yellow and hot red; thus *my* taste wants it; it mixes blood into all colors. But whoever whitewashes his house betrays a whitewashed soul to me. Some in love with mummies, the others with ghosts, and both alike enemies of all flesh and blood—oh, how both offend my taste. For I love blood.

And I do not want to reside and abide where everybody spits and spews: that happens to be *my* taste; rather I would live even among thieves and perjurers. Nobody has gold in his mouth. Still more revolting, however, I find all lickspittles; and the most revolting human animal that I found I baptized "parasite": it did not want to love and yet it wanted to live on love.

Cursed I call all who have only one choice: to become evil beasts or evil tamers of beasts; among such men I would not build my home.

Cursed I call those too who must always *wait*; they offend my taste: all the publicans and shopkeepers and kings and other land- and storekeepers. Verily, I too have learned to wait—thoroughly—but only to wait for *myself*. And above all I learned to stand and walk and jump and climb and dance. This, however, is my doctrine: he who would learn to fly one day must first learn to stand and walk and run and climb and dance: one cannot fly into flying. With rope ladders I have learned to climb to many a window; with swift legs I climbed high masts; and to sit on high masts of knowledge seemed to me no small happiness: to flicker like small flames on high masts—a small light only and yet a great comfort for shipwrecked sailors and castaways.

By many ways, in many ways, I reached my truth: it was not on one ladder that I climbed to the height where my eye roams over my distance. And it was only reluctantly that I ever inquired about the way: that always offended my taste. I preferred to question and try out the ways themselves.

A trying and questioning was my every move; and verily, one must also learn to answer such questioning. That, however, is my taste—not good, not bad, but *my* taste of which I am no longer ashamed and which I have no wish to hide.

"This is *my* way; where is yours?"—thus I answered those who asked me "the way." For *the* way—that does not exist.

"The way" is never to be prescribed for the individual —or for the student. Only through resolute choice (or resolve) can the self be integrated and authentic existence achieved. Confronting manifold possibilities, the person takes into account the actualities of his past and his present situation; and he chooses in the light of what he determines his own potentialities—and his own world, as he understands it—to be. Also, he chooses with an awareness of his temporality and finitude. He lives from instant to instant in a world in which he was cast; only

as he projects himself into the future, and confirms himself through resolutions of conflicting possibilities, can he find a unified "way."

MARTIN HEIDEGGER

Conversation on a Country Path

TEACHER: . . . on our own we do not awaken releasement in ourselves.

SCIENTIST: Thus releasement is effected from somewhere else.

TEACHER: Not effected, but let in.

SCHOLAR: To be sure I don't know yet what the word releasement means, but I seem to presage that releasement awakens when our nature is let-in so as to have dealings with that which is not a willing.

SCIENTIST: You speak without letup of a letting-be and give the impression that what is meant is a kind of passivity. All the same, I think I understand that it is in no way a matter of weakly allowing things to slide and drift along.

SCHOLAR: Perhaps a higher acting is concealed in releasement than is found in all the actions within the world and all the machinations of mankind. . . .

Memorial Address

Yet releasement toward things and openness to the mystery never happen of themselves. They do not befall us accidentally. Both flourish only through persistent, courageous thinking. . . .

If releasement toward things and openness to the mystery awaken within us, then we should arrive at a path that will lead to a new ground and foundation. In that ground the creativity which produces lasting works could strike new roots.

Thus in a different manner and in a changed age, the truth of what Johann Peter Hebel says should be renewed: "We are plants which—whether we like to admit it to ourselves or not—must with our roots rise out of the earth in order to bloom in the ether and to bear fruit."

PAUL TILLICH

The Courage to Be

Vitality, power of life, is correlated to the kind of life to which it gives power. The power of man's life cannot be seen separately from what the medieval philosophers called "intentionality," the relation to meanings. Man's vitality is as great as his intentionality; they are interdependent. This makes man the most vital of all beings. He can transcend any given situation in any direction and this possibility drives him to create beyond himself. Vitality is the power of creating beyond oneself without losing oneself. The more power of creating beyond itself a being has the more vitality it has. The world of technical creations is the most conspicuous expression of man's vitality and its infinite superiority over animal vitality. Only man has complete vitality because he alone has complete intentionality.

We have defined intentionality as "being directed toward meaningful contents." Man lives "in" meanings, in that which is valid logically, esthetically, ethically, religiously. His subjectivity is impregnated with objectivity. In every encounter with reality the structures of self and world are interdependently present. The most fundamental expression of this fact is the language which gives man the power to abstract from the concretely given and, after having abstracted from it, to return to it, to interpret and transform it. The most vital being is the being which has the word and is by the word liberated from bondage to the given. In every encounter with reality, man is already beyond this encounter. He knows about it, he compares it, he is tempted by other possibilities, he anticipates the future as he remembers the past. This is his freedom, and in this freedom the power of his life consists. It is the source of his vitality.

JEAN-PAUL SARTRE

Existentialism

The existentialist . . . thinks it very distressing that God does not exist, because all possibility of finding values in a heaven of ideas disappears along with Him; there can no longer be any *a priori* Good, since there is no infinite and perfect consciousness to think it. Nowhere is it written that the Good exists, that we must be honest, that we must not lie; because the fact is we are on a plane where there are only men. Dostoievsky said, "If God didn't exist, everything would be possible." That is the very starting point of existentialism. Indeed, everything is permissible if God does not exist, and as a result man is forlorn, because neither within him nor without does he find anything to cling to. He can't start making excuses for himself.

If existence really does precede essence, there is no explaining things away by reference to a fixed and given human nature. In other words, there is no determinism, man is free, man is freedom. On the other hand, if God does not exist, we find no values or commands to turn to which legitimize our conduct. So, in the bright realm of values, we have no excuse behind us, nor justification before us. We are alone, with no excuses.

That is the idea I shall try to convey when I say that man is condemned to be free. Condemned, because he did not create himself, yet, in other respects is free; because, once thrown into the world, he is responsible for everything he does. The existentialist does not believe in the power of passion. He will never agree that a sweeping passion is a ravaging torrent which fatally leads a man to certain acts and is therefore an excuse. He thinks that man is responsible for his passion.

The existentialist does not think that man is going to help himself by finding in the world some omen by which to orient himself. Because he thinks that man will interpret the omen to suit himself. Therefore, he thinks that man, with no support and no aid, is condemned every moment to invent man. Ponge, in a very fine article, has said, "Man is the future of man." That's exactly it. But if it is taken to mean that, whatever a man may be, there is a future to be forged, a virgin future before him, then this remark is sound. But then we are forlorn.

To give you an example which will enable you to understand forlornness better, I shall cite the case of one of my students who came to see me under the following circumstances: his father was on bad terms with his mother, and, moreover, was inclined to be a collaborationist; his older brother had been killed in the German offensive of 1940, and the young man, with somewhat immature but generous feelings, wanted to avenge him. His mother lived alone with him, very much upset by the half-treason of her husband and the death of her older son; the boy was her only consolation.

The boy was faced with the choice of leaving for England and joining the Free French Forces—that is, leaving his mother behind—or remaining with his mother and helping her to carry on. He was fully aware that the woman lived only for him and that his going-off—and perhaps his death—would plunge her into despair. He was also aware that every act that he did for his mother's sake was a sure thing, in the sense that it was helping her to carry on, whereas every effort he made toward going off and fighting was an uncertain move which might run aground and prove completely useless; for example, on his way to England he might, while passing through Spain, be detained indefinitely in a Spanish camp; he might reach England or Algiers and be stuck in an office at a desk job. As a result he was faced with two very different kinds of action: one, concrete, immediate, but concerning only one individual; the other concerned an incomparably vaster group, a national collectivity, but for that very reason was dubious, and might be interrupted en route. And, at the same time, he was wavering between two kinds of ethics. On the one hand, an ethics of sympathy, of personal devotion; on the other, a broader ethics, but one whose efficacy was more dubious. He had to choose between the two.

Who could help him choose? Christian doctrine? No. Christian doctrine says, "Be charitable, love your neighbor, take the more rugged path, etc. etc." But which is the more rugged path? Whom should he love as a brother? The fighting man or his mother? Which does the greater good, the vague act of fighting in a group, or the concrete one of helping a particular human being go on living? Who can decide *a priori*? Nobody. No book of ethics can tell him. The Kantian ethics says, "Never treat any person as a means, but as an end." Very well, if I stay with my mother, I'll treat her as an end and not as a means; but by virtue of this very fact, I'm running the risk of treating the people around me who are fighting, as means; and, conversely, if I go to join those who are fighting I'll be treating them as an end, and, by doing that, I run the risk of treating my mother as a means.

If values are vague, and if they are always too broad for the concrete and specific case that we are considering, the only thing left for us is to trust our instincts. That's what this young man tried to do; and when I saw him, he said, "In the end, feeling is what counts. I ought to choose whichever pushes me in one direction. If I feel that I love my mother enough to sacrifice everything else for her—my desire for vengeance, for action, for adventure—then I'll stay with her. If, on the contrary, I feel that my love for my mother isn't enough, I'll leave."

But how is the value of a feeling determined? What

gives his feeling for his mother value? Precisely the fact
that he remained with her. I may say that I like so-and-so
well enough to sacrifice a certain amount of money for
him, but I may say so only if I've done it. I may say
"I love my mother well enough to remain with her" if
I have remained with her. The only way to determine
the value of this affection is, precisely, to perform an
act which confirms and defines it . . . the feeling is
formed by the acts one performs; so, I can not refer to it
in order to act upon it. Which means that I can neither
seek within myself the true condition which will impel
me to act, nor apply to a system of ethics for concepts
which will permit me to act. . . .

. . . Now, for the existentialist there is really no love
other than one which manifests itself in a person's being
in love. There is no genius other than one which is
expressed in works of art. . . . A man is involved in life,
leaves his impress on it, and outside of that there is
nothing. To be sure, this may seem a harsh thought to
someone whose life hasn't been a success. But, on the
other hand, it prompts people to understand that reality
alone is what counts, that dreams, expectations, and
hopes warrant no more than to define a man as a disap-
pointed dream, as miscarried hopes, as vain expectations.
In other words, to define him negatively and not positively. However, when we say, "You are nothing else
than your life," that does not imply that the artist will
be judged solely on the basis of his works of art; a thousand other things will contribute toward summing him
up. What we mean is that man is nothing else than a
series of undertakings, that he is the sum, the organization, the ensemble of the relationships which make up
these undertakings.

*The individual, caught in a world of mere fact, mere
circumstance, must render that world significant by trying to transcend his own facticity. He does this as he
projects himself forward in his utter freedom. He does it*

as he makes himself different from what he is by choosing himself in particular ways. As he makes his choices, he brings values into being for himself, values for which he alone is responsible. There is, however, always a kind of dread involved, always a tendency to pull back and give way to inertia, to what is.

The Age of Reason

. . . Mathieu went up to the window and leaned his elbows on the balcony. He thought: "I *could* not accept," and the room was behind him like a placid sheet of water, only his head emerged above the water, the insidious room was behind him, he kept his head above the water, he looked down into the street, thinking: "Is it true? Is it true I couldn't accept?" In the distance a little girl was skipping; the rope swung above her head like the handle of a basket and whipped the ground beneath her feet. A summer afternoon; the light spanned the street and the roofs, serene and smooth and cold, like an eternal verity. "Is it true I'm not a rotter? The armchair is green, the skipping-rope is like a basket-handle, that's beyond dispute. But where people are concerned, there's always matter for dispute, everything they do can be explained, from above or from below, according to choice. I refused because I wanted to remain free: that's what I can say. And I can also say I was a coward. I like my green curtains, I like to take the air in the evening on my balcony, and I don't want any change. I enjoy railing against capitalism, and I don't want it suppressed, because I should no longer have any reasons for doing so, I enjoy feeling fastidious and aloof. I enjoy saying no, always no, and I should be afraid of any attempt to construct a finally habitable world, because I should merely have to say yes and act like other people. From above or below: who would decide? Brunet has decided: he thinks I am a rotter. So does Jacques; so does Daniel; they have all decided I'm a rotter. Poor Mathieu, he's a wash-out, a rotter. And how can I prevail against them all? I must decide, but what am I to decide?" When he had said no just now, he thought himself sincere, a bitter enthusiasm had suddenly arisen in his heart. But who, beneath that light, could have retained the smallest particle of enthusiasm? It was a light that extinguished hope, that eternalized everything it touched. The little girl would skip forever, the rope would forever swing above her head and forever whip the sidewalk beneath her feet, and Mathieu would look at her forever.

What was the use of skipping? What indeed! What was the use of choosing freedom? Under the same light, at Madrid, at Valencia, men were standing at their windows looking at deserted and eternal streets, and saying, "What's the use? What's the use of continuing the struggle?" Mathieu went back into the room, but the light pursued him there. "*My* armchair, *my* furniture." On the table there was a paperweight in the form of a crab. Mathieu picked it up by the back, as though it were alive. "*My* paperweight." What was the use? What was the use? He dropped the crab on the table and said emphatically to himself: "I am a lousy wash-out."

There is always a certain amount of bad conscience ("I am a lousy wash-out") when a person refuses to choose among the possibilities he confronts. Even in an ordinary classroom, faced with a finite amount of subject matter to be learned, the student may be conscious of an indefinite number of existential possibilities in his concrete life situation. He must somehow be able to rehearse the possibilities that seem to lie ahead in his future; he must be able to appraise himself, to see himself, in various guises, in various roles. Anxiety will be inevitable when he confronts that open future. Yet he must be left to his own devices, to make his own authentic choice and act upon it responsibly. And, finally, the only test of whether he chose correctly or not will be the degree of the authenticity he achieves—the degree of his "good faith."

Being and Nothingness

. . . the one who practices bad faith is hiding a displeasing truth or presenting as truth a pleasing untruth. Bad faith then has in appearance the structure of falsehood. Only what changes everything is the fact that in bad faith it is from myself that I am hiding the truth. Thus the duality of the deceiver and the deceived does not exist here. Bad faith on the contrary implies in essence the unity of a *single* consciousness. . . . One does not undergo his bad faith; one is not infected with it; it is not a *state*. But consciousness affects itself with bad faith. It follows first that the one to whom the lie is told and the one who lies are one and the same person, which means that I must know in my capacity as deceiver the truth which is hidden from me in my capacity as the one deceived. Better yet I must know the truth very exactly *in order* to conceal it more carefully—this not at two different moments, which at a pinch would allow us to reestablish a semblance of duality—but in the unitary structure of a single project. How then can the lie subsist if the duality which conditions it is suppressed?

.   .   .

PATTERNS OF BAD FAITH

If we wish to get out of this difficulty, we should examine more closely the patterns of bad faith and attempt a description of them. This description will permit us perhaps to fix more exactly the conditions for the possibility of bad faith; that is, to reply to the question we raised at the outset: "What must be the being of man if he is to be capable of bad faith?"

Take the example of a woman who has consented to

go out with a particular man for the first time. She knows very well the intentions which the man who is speaking to her cherishes regarding her. She knows also that it will be necessary sooner or later for her to make a decision. But she does not want to realize the urgency; she concerns herself only with what is respectful and discreet in the attitude of her companion. She does not apprehend this conduct as an attempt to achieve what we call "the first approach," that is, she does not want to see possibilities of temporal development which his conduct presents. She restricts this behavior to what is in the present; she does not wish to read in the phrases which he addresses to her anything other than their explicit meaning. . . . The man who is speaking to her appears to her sincere and respectful as the table is round or square, as the wall coloring is blue or gray. The qualities thus attached to the person she is listening to are in this way fixed in a permanence like that of things, which is no other than the projection of the strict present of the qualities into the temporal flux. This is because she does not quite know what she wants. She is profoundly aware of the desire which she inspires, but the desire cruel and naked would humiliate and horrify her. Yet she would find no charm in a respect which would be only respect. In order to satisfy her, there must be a feeling which is addressed wholly to her *personality*—i.e., to her full freedom—and which would be a recognition of her freedom. But at the same time this feeling must be wholly desire; that is, it must address itself to her body as object. This time then she refuses to apprehend the desire for what it is; she does not even give it a name; she recognizes it only to the extent that it transcends itself toward admiration, esteem, respect and that it is wholly absorbed in the more refined forms which it produces, to the extent of no longer figuring anymore as a sort of warmth and density. But then suppose he takes her hand. This act of her companion risks changing the situation by calling for an immediate decision. To leave the hand there is to consent in herself to flirt, to engage herself. To withdraw it is to break the troubled and unstable harmony which gives the hour its charm. The aim is to postpone the moment of decision as long as possible. We know what happens next; the young woman leaves her hand there, but she *does not notice* that she is leaving it. She does not notice because it happens by chance that she is at this moment all intellect. She draws her companion up to the most lofty regions of sentimental speculation; she speaks of Life, of her life, she shows herself in her essential aspect—a personality, a consciousness. And during this time the divorce of the body from the soul is accomplished; the hand rests inert between the warm hands of her companion—neither consenting nor resisting—a thing.

We shall say that this woman is in bad faith. But we see immediately that she uses various procedures in order to maintain herself in bad faith. She has disarmed the actions of her companion by reducing them to being only what they are; that is, to existing in the mode of the in-itself. But she permits herself to enjoy his desire, to the extent that she will apprehend it as not being what it is, will recognize its transcendence. Finally, while sensing profoundly the presence of her own body—to the degree of being disturbed perhaps—she realizes herself as *not being* her own body, and she contemplates it as though from above, as a passive object to which events can *happen* but which can neither provoke them nor avoid them because all its possibilities are outside it. What unity do we find in these various aspects of bad faith? It is a certain art of forming contradictory concepts which unite in themselves both an idea and the negation of that idea. The basic concept which is thus engendered, utilizes the double property of the human being, who is at once a *facticity* and a *transcendence*. These two aspects of human reality are and ought to be capable of a valid coordination. But bad faith does not wish either to coordinate them nor to surmount them in a synthesis. Bad faith seeks to affirm their identity while preserving their differences. It must affirm facticity as *being* transcendence and transcendence as *being* facticity, in such a way that at the instant when a person apprehends the one, he can find himself abruptly faced with the other.

. . . But although this . . . concept of "transcendence-facticity" is one of the most basic instruments of bad faith, it is not the only one of its kind. We can equally well use another kind of duplicity derived from human reality which we will express roughly by saying that its being-for-itself implies complementarily a being-for-others. Upon any one of my conducts it is always possible to converge two looks, mine and that of the Other. The conduct will not present exactly the same structure in each case. But . . . as each look perceives it, there is between these two aspects of my being, no difference between appearance and being—as if I were to my self the truth of myself and as if the Other possessed only a deformed image of me. The equal dignity of being, possessed by my being-for-others and by my being-for-myself permits a perpetually disintegrating synthesis and a perpetual game of escape from the for-itself to the for-others and from the for-others to the for-itself. We have seen also the use to which our young lady made of our being-in-the-midst-of-the-world—i.e., of our inert presence as a passive object among other objects—in order to relieve herself suddenly from the functions of her being-in-the-world—that is, from the being which causes there to be a world by projecting itself beyond the world toward its own possibilities. Let us note finally the confusing syntheses which play on the nihilating ambiguity of these temporal *ekstases* (i.e., moments of separation of for-itself from the Self) affirming at once that I am what I have been (the man who deliberately arrests himself at one period of his life and refuses to take into consideration the later changes) and that I am not what I have been (the man who in the face of reproaches or rancor dissociates himself from his past by insisting on his freedom and on his perpetual re-creation). In all these concepts . . . we find again the same structure. We have to deal with human reality as a being which is what it is not and which is not what it is.

But what exactly is necessary in order for these concepts of disintegration to be able to receive even a pretence of existence, in order for them to be able to appear for an instant to consciousness, even in a process of evanescence? A quick examination of the idea of sincerity, the antithesis of bad faith, will be very instructive in this connection. Actually sincerity presents itself as a demand and consequently is not a state. Now what is the ideal to be attained in this case? It is necessary that a man be *for himself* only what he *is*. But is this not precisely the definition of the in-itself—or if you prefer—the principle of identity? To posit as an ideal the being of things, is this not to assert by the same stroke that this being does not belong to human reality and that the principle of identity, far from being a universal axiom universally applied, is only a synthetic principle enjoying a merely regional universality? Thus in order that the concepts of bad faith can put us under illusion at least for an instant, in order that the candor of "pure hearts" . . . can have validity for human reality as an ideal, the principle of identity must not represent a constitutive principle of human reality and human reality must not be necessarily what it is but must be able to be what it is not. What does this mean?

If man is what he is, bad faith is for ever impossible and candor ceases to be his ideal and becomes instead his being. But *is* man what he is? And more generally, how can he *be* what he is when he exists as consciousness of being? If candor or sincerity is a universal value, it is evident that the maxim "one must be what one is" does not serve solely as a regulating principle for judgements and concepts by which I express what I am. It posits not merely an ideal of knowing but an ideal of *being*; it proposes for us an absolute equivalence of being with itself as a prototype of being. In this sense it is necessary that we *make ourselves* what we are. But what are we then if we have the constant obligation to make ourselves what we are, if our mode of being is having the obligation to be what we are?

Let us consider this waiter in the café. His movement is quick and forward, a little too precise, a little too rapid. He comes toward the patrons with a step a little too quick. He bends forward a little too eagerly; his voice, his eyes express an interest a little too solicitous for the order of the customer. Finally there he returns, trying to imitate in his walk the inflexible stiffness of some kind of automaton while carrying his tray with the recklessness of a tight-rope-walker by putting it in a perpetually unstable, perpetually broken equilibrium which he perpetually reestablishes by a light movement of the arm and hand. All his behavior seems to us a game. He applies himself to chaining his movements as if they were mechanisms, the one regulating the other; his gestures and even his voice seem to be mechanisms; he gives himself the quickness and pitiless rapidity of things. He is playing, he is amusing himself. But what is he playing? We need not watch long before we can explain it: he is playing at being a waiter in a café. There is nothing there to surprise us. The game is a kind of marking out and investigation. The child plays with his body in order to explore it, to take inventory of it; the waiter in the cafe plays with his condition in order to realize it. This obligation is not different from that which is imposed on all tradesmen. Their condition is wholly one of ceremony. The public demands of them that they realize it as a ceremony; there is the dance of the grocer, of the tailor, of the auctioneer, by which they endeavour to persuade their clientele that they are nothing but a grocer, a tailor, an auctioneer. . . . There are indeed many precautions to imprison a man in what he is, as if we lived in perpetual fear that he might escape from it, that he might break away and suddenly elude his condition.

In a parallel situation, from within, the waiter in the café can not be immediately a café waiter in the sense that this inkwell is an inkwell, or the glass is a glass. It is by no means that he can not form reflective judgements or concepts concerning his condition. He knows well what it "means": the obligation of getting up at five o'clock, of sweeping the floor of the shop before the restaurant opens, of starting the coffee pot going, etc. He knows the rights which it allows: the right to the tips, the right to belong to a union, etc. But all these concepts, all these judgements refer to the transcendent. It is a matter of abstract possibilities, of rights and duties conferred on a "person possessing rights." And it is precisely this person *who I have to be* (if I am the waiter in question) and who I am not. It is not that I do not wish to be this person or that I want this person to be different. But rather there is no common measure between his being and mine. It is a "representation" for others and for myself, which means that I can be he only *in representation*. But if I represent myself as him, I am not he; I am separated from him as the object from the subject, separated by *nothing*, but this *nothing* isolates me from him. I can not be he, I can only play at being him; that is, imagine to myself that I am he. And thereby I affect him with nothingness. In vain, do I fulfill the functions of a cafe waiter. I can be he only in the neutralized mode, as the actor is Hamlet, by mechanically making the *typical* gestures of my state and by aiming at myself as an imaginary cafe waiter through those gestures taken as an analogue. What I attempt to realize is a being-in-itself of the cafe waiter, as if it were not just in my power to confer their value and their urgency upon my duties and the rights of my position, as if it were not my free choice to get up each morning at five o'clock or to remain in bed, even though it meant getting fired. As if from the very fact that I sustain this role in existence, I did not transcend it on every side, as if I did not constitute myself as one beyond my condition. Yet there is no doubt that I *am* in a sense a café waiter—otherwise could I not just as well call myself a diplomat or a reporter? But if I am one, this can not be in the mode of being-in-itself. I am a waiter in the mode of being-what-I-am-not.

Furthermore we are dealing with more than mere social position; I am never any one of my attitudes, any one of my actions. The good speaker is the one who *plays* at speaking, because he can not *be* speaking. The attentive pupil who wishes to *be* attentive, his eyes riveted on the teacher, his ears open wide, so exhausts himself in playing the attentive role that he ends up by no longer hearing anything. Perpetually absent to my body, to my acts, I am despite myself that "divine absence" of which Valery speaks. I can not say either that I am here or that I am not here, in the sense that we say "that box of matches *is* on the table"; this would be to confuse my "being-in-the-world" with a "being in the midst of the world." . . .

Caught up in the details and contingencies of school life and life outside of school, the young person is very likely to evade his own freedom and the responsibility it entails. In a "spirit of seriousness," he is likely to perceive values as "given," inhering in the things and institutions of his world. Involved in the immediate, the everyday, he may become passive with respect to what is said to be of worth and avoid the recognition that he is the creator of his values, and that in order to create them, he must transcend the routine immediacies. He must experience the anxiety, in other words, that comes with the rejection of habitual expectations, the rejection of other people's identifications of who he is and what he is scheduled to be.

ALBERT CAMUS

Preface to *The Stranger*

In our society a man who doesn't weep at his mother's
funeral runs the risk of being condemned to death. . . .
Meursault doesn't play the game. . . . In this sense, he
is a stranger to the society on whose outskirts he wan-
ders, living his own private, lonely, sensual life. . . .
. . . he refuses to lie. Now, lying is not only saying
what is not. It's also saying more than is, and in matters
of the human heart, more than we feel. We all do this
every day, in order to simplify life. Meursault, contrary
to appearances, does not want to simplify life. He tells
the truth, he refuses to exaggerate his feelings, and immediately society feels itself threatened. For instance, he
is asked to say that he is sorry for his crime, according to
the conventional formula. He answers that he experiences
more annoyance on its account than genuine sorrow. And
this nuance condemns him. . . .

*Meursault's is a negative truth, but he remains in good
faith. And when he finally confronts the full "absurdity"
of his condemnation, he makes a choice—perhaps the
first significant choice of his life. Choosing, he creates
the values by which he has lived and by which he will
die. But he has been moved to create these values and
to impose a meaning on his life by the recognition of his
problematic freedom, a recognition required of all who
are intent on living in good faith and remaining free to
choose.*

The Stranger

Then, I don't know how it was, but something seemed
to break inside me, and I started yelling at the top of
my voice. I hurled insults at him, I told him not to

waste his rotten prayers on me; it was better to burn
than to disappear. I'd taken him by the neckband of his
cassock, and, in a sort of ecstasy of joy and rage, I
poured out on him all the thoughts that had been sim-
mering in my brain. He seemed so cocksure, you see. And
yet none of his certainties was worth one strand of a
woman's hair. Living as he did, like a corpse, he couldn't
even be sure of being alive. It might look as if my hands
were empty. Actually, I was sure of myself, sure about
everything, far surer than he; sure of my present life
and of the death that was coming. That, no doubt, was
all I had; but at least that certainty was something I
could get my teeth into—just as it had got its teeth into
me. I'd been right, I was still right, I was always right.
I'd passed my life in a certain way, and I might have
passed it in a different way, if I'd felt like it. I'd acted
thus, and I hadn't acted otherwise; I hadn't done *x*,
whereas I had done *y* or *z*. And what did that mean?
That, all the time, I'd been waiting for this present moment, for that dawn, tomorrow's or another day's, which
was to justify me. Nothing, nothing had the least importance, and I knew quite well why. He, too, knew
why. From the dark horizon of my future a sort of slow,
persistent breeze had been blowing toward me, all my
life long, from the years that were to come. And on its
way that breeze had leveled out all the ideas that people
tried to foist on me in the equally unreal years I then
was living through. What difference could they make to
me, the deaths of others, or a mother's love, or his God;
or the way a man decides to live, the fate he thinks he
chooses, since one and the same fate was bound to
"choose" not only me but thousands of millions of privileged people who, like him, called themselves my brothers. Surely, surely he must see that? Every man alive
was privileged; there was only one class of men, the
privileged class. All alike would be condemned to die
one day; his turn, too, would come like the others'. And
what difference could it make if, after being charged with
murder, he were executed because he didn't weep at his

mother's funeral, since it all came to the same thing in
the end? The same thing for Salamano's wife and for
Salamano's dog. That little robot woman was as "guilty"
as the girl from Paris who had married Masson, or as
Marie, who wanted me to marry her. What did it matter
if Raymond was as much my pal as Céleste, who was a
far worthier man? What did it matter if at this very
moment Marie was kissing a new boy friend? As a condemned man himself, couldn't he grasp what I meant
by that dark wind blowing from my future? . . .

. . . I, too, felt ready to start life all over again. It
was as if that great rush of anger had washed me clean,
emptied me of hope, and, gazing up at the dark sky
spangled with its signs and stars, for the first time, the
first, I laid my heart open to the benign indifference of
the universe. To feel it so like myself, indeed, so broth-
erly, made me realize that I'd been happy, and that I
was happy still. . . .

*Meursault never transcended his own engagement with
immediacies, his love for "that sun which casts no
shadows"; and his "truth," important as it is, remains
negative. He has lived, as it were, "aesthetically," without attachment, without commitment. The individual
who lives ethically cannot be indifferent; since indifference is equivalent to giving way to "plague": the mechanisms, injustices, evasions of the world. If young people
are to be liberated to choose themselves and create values,
they too—to the limit of their capacity—ought to be
brought into confrontation.*

The Plague

"Have you ever seen a man shot by a firing squad? No,
of course not; the spectators are hand-picked and it's
like a private party, you need an invitation. The result
is that you've gleaned your ideas about it from books and
pictures. A post, a blind-folded man, some soldiers in the

offing. But the real thing isn't a bit like that. Do you know that the firing squad stands only a yard and a half from the condemned man? Do you know that if the victim took two steps forward his chest would touch the rifles? Do you know that, at short range, the soldiers concentrate their fire on the region of the heart and their big bullets make a hole into which you could thrust your fist? No, you didn't know all that; those are things that are never spoken of. For the plague-stricken their peace of mind is more important than a human life. Decent folks must be allowed to sleep easy o' nights, mustn't they? Really it would be shockingly bad taste to linger on such details, that's common knowledge. But personally I've never been able to sleep well since then. The bad taste remained in my mouth and I've kept lingering on the details, brooding over them.

"And thus I came to understand that I, anyhow, had had plague through all those long years in which, paradoxically enough, I'd believed with all my soul that I was fighting it. I learned that I had had an indirect hand in the deaths of thousands of people; that I'd even brought about their deaths by approving of acts and principles which could only end that way. Others did not seem embarrassed by such thoughts, or anyhow never voiced them of their own accord. But I was different; what I'd come to know stuck in my gorge. I was with them and yet I was alone. . . .

"In any case, my concern was not with arguments. . . . My concern was with that hole in a man's chest. And I told myself that meanwhile, so far anyhow as I was concerned, nothing in the world would induce me to accept any argument that justified such butcheries. Yes, I chose to be blindly obstinate, pending the day when I could see my way more clearly.

"I'm still of the same mind. For many years I've been ashamed, mortally ashamed, of having been, even with the best of intentions, even at many removes, a murderer in my turn. As time went on I merely learned that even those who were better than the rest could not keep them-

selves nowadays from killing or letting others kill, because such is the logic by which they live; and that we
can't stir a finger in this world without the risk of bring-
ing death to somebody. Yes, I've been ashamed ever
since; I have realized that we all have plague, and I
have lost my peace. And today I am still trying to find it;
still trying to understand all those others and not be the
mortal enemy of anyone. I only know that one must do
what one can to cease being plague-stricken, and that's
the only way in which we can hope for some peace, or,
failing that, a decent death. This, and only this, can
bring relief to men and, if not save them, at least do
them the least harm possible and even, sometimes, a
little good. So that is why I resolved to have no truck
with anything which, directly or indirectly, for good
reasons or for bad, brings death to anyone or justifies
others' putting him to death.

"That, too, is why this epidemic has taught me nothing new, except that I must fight it at your side. I know
positively—yes, Rieux, I can say I know the world inside
out, as you may see—that each of us has the plague
within him; no one, no one on earth is free from it.
And I know, too, that we must keep endless watch on
ourselves lest in a careless moment we breathe in somebody's face and fasten the infection on him. What's
natural is the microbe. All the rest—health, integrity,
purity (if you like)—is a product of the human will, of
a vigilance that must never falter. The good man, the
man who infects hardly anyone, is the man who has the
fewest lapses of attention. And it needs tremendous will-
power, a never ending tension of the mind, to avoid such
lapses. Yes, Rieux, it's a wearying business, being plague-
stricken. But it's still more wearying to refuse to be it.
That's why everybody in the world today looks so tired;
everyone is more or less sick of plague. But that is also
why some of us, those of us who want to get the plague
out of their systems, feel such desperate weariness, a
weariness from which nothing remains to set us free
except death.

"Pending that release, I know I have no place in the world of today; once I'd definitely refused to kill, I doomed myself to an exile that can never end. I leave it to others to make history. I know, too, that I'm not qualified to pass judgement on those others. There's something lacking in my mental make-up, and its lack prevents me from being a rational murderer. So it's a deficiency, not a superiority. But as things are, I'm willing to be as I am; I've learned modesty. All I maintain is that on this earth there are pestilences and there are victims, and it's up to us, so far as possible, not to join forces with the pestilences. That may sound simple to the point of childishness; I can't judge if it's simple, but I know it's true. You see, I'd heard such quantities of arguments, which very nearly turned my head, and turned other people's heads enough to make them approve of murder; and I'd come to realize that all our troubles spring from our failure to use plain, clear-cut language. So I resolved always to speak—and to act—quite clearly, as this was the only way of setting myself on the right track. That's why I say there are pestilences and there are victims; no more than that. If, by making that statement, I, too, become a carrier of the plague-germ, at least I don't do it willfully. I try, in short, to be an innocent murderer. I've no great ambitions."

The situations into which human beings are cast are multiple. They range from the "Euclidian universe" to the paradoxical and "absurd," and from there to the "environment" of brute existences and menacing "things." They include objects, tools, and other human beings; and at their "boundaries" they verge on nothingness, on the "Encompassing," on Being, or on God. However described, they must be experienced inwardly by each individual, each Dasein, each being-in-the-world; and each living subject must effect his own authentic relationships with the situations he encounters throughout the "instants" of his life. There is, in consequence, something irreducibly problematic about the situation in which true learning takes place. The everyday, the ordinary are in some sense disrupted; the questioning student must break with the ready-made, with conventional wisdom; he must choose himself as a conscious being—choose himself to know.

SOREN KIERKEGAARD

Either / Or

Let others complain that the age is wicked; my complaint is that it is wretched, for it lacks passion. Men's thoughts are thin and flimsy like lace, they are themselves pitiable like the lacemakers. The thoughts of their hearts are too paltry to be sinful. For a worm it might be regarded as a sin to harbor such thoughts, but not for a being made in the image of God. Their lusts are dull and sluggish, their passions sleepy. They do their duty, these shop-keeping souls, but they clip the coin a trifle. . . . Out upon them! This is the reason my soul always turns back to the Old Testament and to Shakespeare. I feel that those who speak there are at least human beings: they hate, they love, they murder their enemies, and curse their descendants throughout all generations, they sin.

.   .   .

My grief is my castle, which like an eagle's nest is built high upon the mountain peaks among the clouds; nothing can storm it. From it I fly down into reality to seize my prey; but I do not remain down there, I bring it home with me, and this prey is a picture I weave into the tapestries of my palace. There I live as one dead. I immerse everything I have experienced in a baptism of forgetfulness unto an eternal remembrance. Everything finite and accidental is forgotten and erased. Then I sit like an old man, grey-haired and thoughtful, and explain the pictures in a voice as soft as a whisper; and at my side a child sits and listens, although he remembers every-thing before I tell it.

Men have no passion when they do not yearn to be-come, when they refuse to aspire after the infinite. This is the complacency of middle-class security, which forces the existential thinker into estrangement. But, in his es-trangement and in the "grief" he feels, he is choosing the crisis through which he can move to authentic life.

Concluding Unscientific Postscript

It is now about four years since I got the notion of want-ing to try my hand as an author. I remember it quite

clearly; it was on a Sunday, yes, that's it, a Sunday afternoon. As usual I was sitting out-of-doors at the cafe in
the Frederiksberg Garden, that wonderful garden which
for the child was fairyland, where the King dwelt with
his Queen, that delightful garden which afforded the
youth happy diversion in the merriment of the populace,
that friendly garden where now for the man of riper years
there is such a homely feeling of sad exaltation above
the world and all that is of the world. . . . There I sat
as usual and smoked my cigar . . .

I had been a student for ten years. Although never
lazy, all my activity nevertheless was like a glittering
inactivity, a kind of occupation for which I still have a
strong predilection, and perhaps even a little talent. I
read much, spent the rest of the day idling and thinking,
or thinking and idling, but that was all it came to; the
earliest sproutings of my productivity barely sufficed for
my daily use and were consumed in their first greening.
An inexplicable and overwhelming might constantly held
me back, by strength as well as by artifice. This might
was my indolence. It is not like the vehement aspiration
of love, nor like the strong incentive of enthusiasm, it is
rather like a housekeeper who holds one back, and with
whom one is very well off, so well off that it never occurs to one to get married. This much is sure: though
with the comforts of life I am not on the whole un-
acquainted, of all, indolence is the most comfortable.

So there I sat and smoked my cigar until I lapsed into
reverie. Among other thoughts I remember this: "You
are now," I said to myself, "on the way to becoming an
old man, without being anything, and without really
undertaking to do anything. On the other hand, wherever you look about you, in literature and in life, you see
the celebrated names and figures, the precious and much
heralded men who are coming into prominence and are
much talked about, the many benefactors of the age who
know how to benefit mankind by making life easier and
easier, some by railways, others by omnibuses and steam-
boats, others by telegraph, others by easily apprehended

compendiums and short recitals of everything worth knowing, and finally the true benefactors of the age who by virtue of thought make spiritual existence systematically easier and easier, and yet more and more significant. And what are you doing?"

Here my self-communion was interrupted, for my cigar was burned out and a new one had to be lit. So I smoked again, and then suddenly there flashed through my mind this thought: "You must do something, but inasmuch as with your limited capacities it will be impossible to make anything easier than it has become, you must, with the same humanitarian enthusiasm as the others, undertake to make something harder." This notion pleased me immensely, and at the same time it flattered me to think that I, like the rest of them, would be loved and esteemed by the whole community. For when all combine in every way to make everything easier and easier, there remains only one possible danger, namely, that the easiness might become so great that it would be too great; then only one want is left, though not yet a felt want—that people will want difficulty. Out of love for mankind, and out of despair at my embarrassing situation, seeing that I had accomplished nothing and was unable to make anything easier than it had already been made, and moved by a genuine interest in those who make everything easy, I conceived it my task to create difficulties everywhere. . . .

The inertia of the person who defends himself against the struggle to be can (with or without irony) be projected into the historical situation. Then, as now, men existed in a situation characterized by a "Public," by anonymity and irresponsibility, as well as by great technical progress. The existential thinker recognizes the importance of history as a study of the past; but even more important is history understood as "historicity"—or an approach to the past as possibility, a projection de-

manding constant repetition or the continual appropriation of what has been in order to make it presently significant. It becomes significant as it is taken over in moments of choice. And the self, committed to making "something harder," becomes engaged in realizing its own past in its own future, acting to transcend itself.

FRIEDRICH NIETZSCHE

The Genealogy of Morals, XII

. . . Exactly what is it that I, especially, find intolerable; that I am unable to cope with, that asphyxiates me? A bad smell. The smell of failure, of a soul that has gone stale. God knows it is possible to endure all kinds of misery—vile weather, sickness, trouble, isolation. All this can be coped with, if one is born to a life of anonymity and battle. There will always be moments of reemergence into the light, when one tastes the golden hour of victory and once again stands foursquare, unshakable, ready to face even harder things, like a bowstring drawn taut against new perils. But, you divine patronesses—if there are any such in the realm beyond good and evil —grant me now and again the sight of something perfect, wholly achieved, happy, magnificently triumphant, something still capable of inspiring fear! Of a man who will justify the existence of mankind, for whose sake one may continue to believe in mankind! . . . The leveling and diminution of European man is our greatest danger; because the sight of him makes us despond. . . . We no longer see anything these days that aspires to grow greater; instead, we have a suspicion that things will continue to go downhill, becoming ever thinner, more placid, smarter, cosier, more ordinary, more indifferent, more Chinese, more Christian—without doubt man is getting "better" all the time . . . This is Europe's true predicament: together with the fear of man we have also lost the love of man, reverence for man, confidence in man, indeed the *will to man*. Now the sight of man makes us despond. What is nihilism today if not that?

RAINER MARIA RILKE

The Neighbor

Strange violin, are you following me?
In how many towns when I am alone
your lonely night has called to mine?
Do hundreds play you, or only one?

Are there in all great cities ever
those who without you would have lost
themselves already in the river?
Will your music pick on me to the last?

Why must I always have as neighbor
him who makes you so fearfully sing
and say that life is heavier
than the heaviness of all things?

FRANZ KAFKA

Aphorisms

He feels imprisoned on this earth, he feels constricted; the melancholy, the impotence, the sicknesses, the feverish fancies of the captives afflict him; no comfort can comfort him, since it is merely comfort, gentle headsplitting comfort glozing the brutal fact of imprisonment. But if he is asked what he actually wants he cannot reply, for—that is one of his strongest proofs—he has no conception of freedom.

.   .   .

The sluggish, self-torturing, wavelike motion of all life, whether of other life or his own, which often seems to stagnate for a long time but in reality never ceases, tortures him because it brings with it the never-ceasing compulsion to think. Sometimes it seems to him that this torture heralds events. When he hears that a married friend of his is awaiting the birth of his first child he recognizes that in thought he has already paid the price of that birth.

.   .   .

He fights against having his limits defined by his fellow-men. No man, even if he be infallible, can see more than that fraction of his neighbour for which his strength and kind of vision are adapted. He has, however, like everybody, but in its most extreme form, the longing to limit himself to the limit of his neighbour's eyesight. Had Robinson Crusoe never left the highest, or more correctly the most visible point of his island, from desire for comfort, or timidity, or fear, or ignorance, or longing, he would soon have perished; but since without paying any attention to passing ships and their feeble telescopes he started to explore the whole island and take pleasure in it, he managed to keep himself alive and finally was found after all, by a chain of causality that was, of course, logically inevitable.

.   .   .

The question of conscience is a social imposition. All virtues are individual, all vices social. The things that pass as social virtues, love, for example, disinterestedness, justice, self-sacrifice, are only "astonishingly" enfeebled social vices.

Man, always in-the-world, always caught up in a complex system of relations, is forever in danger of submitting to Das Man—or impersonality, the agent of the customary and conventional, the voice of the "Crowd." There

*may be moments, however, when "dread" overtakes him,
a sudden insight into his own inauthentic life. He is
plunged into "Nothing." Everything to which he has
given intelligibility through his ordinary life and work
becomes abruptly meaningless, and he is thrust back into
pure contingency.*

MARTIN HEIDEGGER

What Is Metaphysics?

But why worry about this Nothing? "Nothing" is absolutely rejected by science and abandoned as null and
void . . .

. . . we postulate Nothing as something that somehow
or other "is"—as an entity. . . . But it is nothing of the
sort. The question as to the what and wherefore of
Nothing turns the thing questioned into its opposite. The
question deprives itself of its own object. . . .

. . . If, however, we refuse to be led astray by the
formal impossibility of an enquiry into Nothing and still
continue to enquire in the face of it, we must at least
satisfy what remains the fundamental pre-requisite for
the full pursuit of any enquiry. If Nothing as such is
still to be enquired into, it follows that it must be "given"
in advance. We must be able to encounter it.

Where shall we seek Nothing? Where shall we find
Nothing? . . . First and foremost we can only look as
if we have presupposed the presence of a thing to be
looked for. But here the thing we are looking for is
Nothing. Is there after all a seeking without presupposi-
tion, a seeking complemented by a pure finding? . . .

. . . Naturally enough it looks as if, in our everyday
activities, we were always holding on to this or that
actuality . . . as if we were lost in this or that region
of what-is. However fragmentary the daily round may
appear it still maintains what-is, in however shadowy a

fashion, within the unity of a "whole." Even when, or rather, precisely when we are not absorbed in things or in our own selves, this "wholeness" comes over us—for example, in real boredom. Real boredom is still far off when this book or that play, this activity, or that stretch of idleness merely bores us. Real boredom comes when "one is bored." This profound boredom, drifting hither and thither in the abysses of existence like a mute fog, draws all things, all men and oneself along with them, together in a queer kind of indifference. This boredom reveals what-is in totality.

There is another possibility of such revelation, and this is in the joy we feel in the presence of the being— not merely the person—of someone we love.

Because of these moods in which, as we say, we "are" this or that, we find ourselves . . . in the midst of what-is-in-totality, wholly pervaded by it. The affective state in which we find ourselves not only discloses, according to the mood we are in, what-is in totality, but this disclosure is at the same time far from being a chance occurrence and is the ground-phenomenon of our Dasein. . . .

. . . Does there ever occur in human existence a mood of this kind, through which we are brought face to face with Nothing itself?

This may and actually does occur, albeit rather seldom and for moments only, in the key-mood of dread (*Angst*) . . . "Dread of" is always a dreadful feeling "about"— but not about this or that. The indefiniteness of *what* we dread is not just lack of definition. . . . The indefiniteness is brought out in an illustration. . . .

In dread, as we say, "one feels something uncanny," What is this "something" and this "one"? . . . All things, and we with them, sink into a sort of indifference. But not in the sense that everything simply disappears; rather, in the very act of drawing away from us everything turns towards us. This withdrawal of what-is-in-totality, which then crowds round us in dread, this is what oppresses us. There is nothing to hold on to. The only thing that remains and overwhelms us whilst what-is slips away is this "nothing."

Dread reveals Nothing.

It is by means of a projection into the situation in which dread descends on the self that the self relates with any degree of consciousness to the what-is. And it is by means of such projection that the questioner begins asking the kind of "why?" to which science can provide answers. In other words, it is largely through awareness of the Not that the individual is shaken out of the false comfort of total intelligibility which accompanies the inauthentic submergence in the world. And it may be that the situations of the "modern" world, haunted and dominated by Das Man, *are particularly likely to lull the individual into the slumber which is a refusal to be.*

MARTIN BUBER

Between Man and Man

. . . And since, as we have seen, the depths of the question about man's being are revealed only to the man who has become solitary, the way to the answer lies through the man who overcomes his solitude without forfeiting its questioning power. This means that a *new* task in life is set to human thought here, a task that is new in its context of *life.* For it means that the man who wants to grasp what he himself is, salvages the tension of solitude and its burning problematic for a life with his world, a life that is renewed in spite of all, and out of this new situation proceeds with his thinking. . . .

. . . Both views of life—modern individualism and modern collectivism—however different their causes may be, are essentially the conclusion or expression of the same human condition, only at different stages. This condition is characterized by the union of cosmic and social homelessness, dread of the universe and dread of life, resulting in an existential constitution of solitude such as probably never existed before to the same extent. The human person feels himself to be a man exposed by nature—as an unwanted child is exposed—and at the same time a person isolated in the midst of the tumultuous human world. The first reaction of the spirit to the awareness of this new and uncanny position is modern individualism, the second is modern collectivism.

In individualism, the human being ventures to affirm his position, to plunge it into an affirmative reflexion, a universal *amor fati;* he wants to build the citadel of a life-system in which the idea asserts that it wills reality as it is. Just because man is exposed by nature, he is an individual in this specially radical way in which no other being in the world is an individual; and he accepts his exposure because it means that he is an individual. In the same way he accepts his isolation as a person, for only a monad which is not bound to others can know and glorify itself as an individual to the utmost. To save himself from the despair with which his solitary state threatens him, man resorts to the expedient of glorifying it. Modern individualism has essentially an imaginary basis. It founders on this character, for imagination is not capable of actually conquering the given situation.

The second reaction, collectivism, essentially follows upon the foundering of the first. Here the human being tries to escape his destiny of solitude by becoming completely embedded in one of the massive modern group formations. The more massive, unbroken and powerful in its achievements this is, the more the man is able to feel that he is saved from both forms of homelessness. . . . There is obviously no further reason for dread of life, since one needs only to fit oneself into the "general will" and let one's own responsibility for an existence which has become all too complicated be absorbed in collective responsibility, which proves itself able to meet all complications. Likewise, there is obviously no further

reason for dread of the universe, since technicized nature
—with which society as such manages well, or seems to—
takes the place of the universe which has become uncanny and with which . . . no further agreement can
be reached. The collective pledges itself to provide total
security. There is nothing imaginary here, a dense reality
rules, and the "general" itself appears to have become
real; but modern collectivism is essentially illusory. The
person is joined to the reliably functioning "whole,"
which embraces the masses of men; but it is not a joining
of man to man . . . Here the person is not freed from
his isolation, by communing with living beings . . . ;
the "whole," with its claims on the wholeness of every
man, aims logically and successfully at reducing, neutral-
izing, devaluating, and desecrating every bond with living
beings. The tender surface of personal life which longs
for contact with other life is progressively deadened and
desensitized. . . . Modern collectivism is the last barrier
raised by man against a meeting with himself.

. . . Life and thought are here placed in the same
problematic situation. As life erroneously supposes that
it has to choose between individualism and collectivism,
so thought erroneously supposes that it has to choose
between an individualistic anthropology and a collectivist
sociology. The genuine third alternative, when it is
found, will point the way . . .

The fundamental fact of human existence is neither
the individual as such nor the aggregate as such. Each,
considered in itself, is a mighty abstraction. The individual is a fact of existence in so far as he steps into a
living relation with other individuals. The aggregate is
a fact of existence in so far as it is built up of living units
of relation. The fundamental fact of human existence is
man with man. What is peculiarly characteristic of the
human world is above all that something takes place between one being and another the like of which can be
found nowhere in nature. Language is only a sign and
a means for it, all achievement of the spirit has been

incited by it. Man is made man by it; but on its way it
does not merely unfold, it also decays and withers away.
It is rooted in one being turning to another as another,
as this particular other being, in order to communicate
with it in a sphere which is common to them but which
reaches out beyond the special sphere of each. I call this
sphere, which is established with the existence of man
as man but which is conceptually still uncomprehended,
the sphere of "between." Though being realized in very
different degrees, it is a primal category of human
reality. This is where the genuine third alternative must
begin.

*Somehow each person in a classroom must be enlisted
and "stirred up" as a person engaged in an ongoing
dialogue. The emphasis must be placed on what happens between those concerned with teaching and learning, on the kind of lesson "which develops in mutual
surprises" rather than transmitting what the teacher has
already "found." This means an emphasis upon the discoveries which take place through and by means of
dialogue and shared endeavor. Only so can isolation be
avoided in the busy, even the "ungraded," classroom;
only so can the existing person be conceived as prior to
the group.*

KARL JASPERS

Man in the Modern Age

. . . When I am still striving to understand the mental
situation of the epoch, I am aspiring to exercise my
faculties as a human being endowed with intelligence;
and as long as my understanding remains incomplete, I
can only think of the situation as working itself out
independently of my contribution; but as soon as I be-

come an active participator in the situation, I want reflectively to interfere with the action and reaction between the situation and my own existence.

We have to ask, however, what sort of situation I mean.

Man's being consists primarily of his existence in economic, sociological, and political situations, upon whose reality everything else depends; perhaps, even, it is only through the reality of these situations that everything else becomes real.

Secondly, man's life as a conscious being lies within the realm of the cognizable. Historically acquired and now extant knowledge (regarded as to its content, its mode of acquisition, and its methodological classification and increase) is situation as the possible lucidity of man's mind.

Thirdly, what a man can himself become is, *qua* situation, determined by the other persons whom he encounters on his journey through life and by the possibilities of belief which appeal to him.

Thus, when I am in search of the mental situation I must take into account actual being, the possible lucidity of knowledge, and the potentialities of belief.

a) As regards his sociological existence, the individual is restricted to a specific environment, and is therefore not to an equal degree a participator in all environments. As yet the elements of a knowledge how man comports himself in all the extant sociological situations, is not available. Indeed, it is probable that few others know much about what, for the individual concerned, seems a matter of course in his daily experience.

Today, doubtless, the individual has more mobility of status than ever before. . . . People have acquired a certain amount of general knowledge regarding the main types of existence, such as that of the wage-earner, the salaried employee, the peasant, the handicraftsman, the entrepreneur, the civil servant. But the general fellowship of our human situation has been rendered even more dubious than before, inasmuch as . . . a new restriction of the individual to some prescribed status in the sociological machinery has become manifest. . . . What is today common to us all is not our humanity as a universal and all-pervading spirit of fellowship, but the cosmopolitanism of catch-words in conjunction with the spread of world-wide means of communication and the universalization of certain pastimes. The general sociological situation is not the decisive factor in our destinies, being, rather, that which threatens us with annihilation. The decisive factor is the developing possibility of a selfhood which is not yet objectively extant—of a selfhood in a particular realm which includes and overrides the general, instead of being included in or overridden by it. This selfhood does not yet exist for contemporary man, but looms as a realisable possibility if man deliberately and successfully intervenes as one of the factors of his own destiny.

b) As far as knowledge is concerned, the contemporary situation signifies the increasing accessibility of form and method, and of many of the elements of science, to a continually increasing number of persons. But as far as the individual is concerned, not only are the attainable limits very different from person to person—this being an objective matter—but also subjectively in most persons the will is not yet ripe, and hence they remain incapable of a spontaneous urge towards fundamental knowledge. From a generalised outlook upon knowledge it might be supposed that an identical situation would be possible for us all as the expression of comprehensive intercommunication which could readily determine the mental situation of all human beings of a particular period after a uniform fashion. But this uniformity is rendered impossible by the discrepancies between us as regards desire for knowledge.

c) Coming now to the relations between one selfhood and another, there is no generalisable situation, but only the absolute historicity of those who encounter one another, the intimacy of their contact, the fidelity and irreplaceability of personal ties. Amid the general social dissolution, man is thrust back into dependence upon these most primitive bonds out of which alone a new and trustworthy objectivity can be constructed.

It is, then, incontestable that there can be no such thing as a homogeneous situation for all human beings of a particular epoch. Were we to conceive the existence of mankind as a sort of unified substance which from age to age found itself in varying specific situations, the imagination would lose itself in the void. . . . I as an individual should, however extensive my knowledge, run my course within the process and could not as a cognitive being stand outside it . . .

. . . The historical picture of universal human development as a necessary process . . . is doubtless fascinating. I am what the time is. But what the time is, discloses itself as a particular phase in the process. If I know this phase, I know what the time demands. To come to grips with existence, I must know the totality through knowing which I learn where we stand today. . . . But the opinion that we can know what the whole, historically, or at this actual moment, really is, is fallacious. The very existence of the alleged whole is questionable. . . . Since my own being has inevitably to play a part in the integrality of existence, independent knowledge is a "pious wish"; it is the sketch of a route I should like to follow; it is resentment which finds an outlet in the animus of such supposititious knowledge; it is passivity which is thereby justified; it is an aesthetic pleasure which I derive from the splendour of my imaginary picture; it is a gesture whereby I can gratify my self-assertive impulse.

Nonetheless in the world of relativity, glimpses of the kind have a use and a meaning—are, indeed, indispensable if we are really to grasp our own situation where we come to venture upon the other and true path which knows naught of a totality. As soon as I have become aware how and by what means and within what limits knowledge is attainable, I have no choice but incessantly to strive towards an understanding of my time and its situations. A knowledge of my world provides the sole means whereby I can: first of all, become aware of the extent of the possible; secondly shape sound plans and form effective resolves; thirdly, acquire the outlooks and ideas that will enable me (a philosopher) to interpret human life as a manifestation of Transcendence.

As a participant in knowledge, the student can only be asked to create his own appropriate orders out of what he learns, orders that derive in part from his sense of his location in time and space, his awareness of his own limitations and his own existential possibilities. "Appropriating" knowledge of the past, the present, and the natural world around him, he becomes increasingly aware of the variety of meanings available to him. Also, he becomes aware of the "boundaries" of the life situation he shares with others. It is in his consciousness of those boundaries, those limits, that he experiences the anxiety —the dread—which generates responsible choice.

JEAN-PAUL SARTRE

The Psychology of Imagination

We shall give the name of "situations" to the different immediate ways of apprehending the real as a world. We can therefore say that the essential prerequisite that enables consciousness to imagine is that it be "situated in the world" or more briefly, that it "be-in-the-world." It is situation-in-the-world, grasped as a concrete and individual reality of consciousness, which is the motivation for the construction of any unreal object whatever and the nature of that unreal object is circumscribed by this motivation. Thus the *situation* of consciousness does not need to appear as a pure and abstract condition of possibility for all imagination but as the concrete and exact motivation for the appearance of a certain particular imagination.

From this point of view we finally grasp the relation between the unreal and the real. At first, even if an image is not produced at this moment, every apprehension of the real as a world tends of its own accord to end up with the production of unreal objects because it is always, in one sense, a free negation of the world and that always *from a particular point of view*. . . . Thus, although as a result of producing the unreal, consciousness can appear momentarily delivered from "being-in-the-world," it is just this "being-in-the-world" which is the necessary condition for the imagination.

Thus the critical analysis of the conditions that made all imagination possible has led us to the following discoveries: in order to imagine, consciousness must be free from all specific reality and this freedom must be able to define itself by a "being-in-the-world" which is at once the constitution and the negation of the world; the concrete situation of the consciousness in the world must at each moment serve as the singular motivation for the constitution of the unreal. Thus the unreal—which is always a two-fold nothingness: nothingness of itself in relation to the world, nothingness of the world in relation to itself—must always be constituted on the foundation of the world which it denies, it being well understood, moreover, that the world does not present itself only to a representative intuition and that this synthetic foundation simply demands to be lived as a situation. If these are the conditions which make imagination possible, do they correspond to a specification, to an enrichment contingent upon the essence "consciousness" or are they nothing else than the very essence of that consciousness considered from a particular point of view? It seems that the answer lies in the question. Indeed, what is this free consciousness whose nature is to be the consciousness of something, but which, for this very reason, constructs itself before the real and which surpasses it at each moment because it can exist only by "being-in-the-world," that is, by living its relation to the real as *situation,* what is it, indeed, if not simply consciousness such as it reveals itself to itself in the cogito? . . .

. . . We may therefore conclude that imagination is not an empirical and superadded power of consciousness, it is the whole of consciousness as it realizes its freedom; every concrete and real situation of consciousness in the world is big with imagination in as much as it always presents itself as a withdrawing from the real. It does not follow that all perception of the real must reverse itself in imagination, but as consciousness is always "in a situation" because it is always free, it always and at each moment has the concrete possibility of producing the unreal.

Truly to live—concretely and freely—within a situation, the individual must be able to "bracket out" the ordinary, the comfortable, the "easy." It is imagination which permits him to bracket in this fashion and which turns him back upon himself. Turned back, he becomes subjectively aware of his own consciousness, of his own freedom. Relating imaginatively to what he now experiences as his situation, he is open to the doubt, the unrest, and the "guilt" which are required if he is to learn.

Being and Nothingness

Every free project in projecting itself anticipates a margin of unpredictability due to the independence of things, precisely because this independence is that in terms of which a freedom is constituted. As soon as I project going to a nearby village to find Pierre, the punctures, the "headwind," a thousand foreseeable and unforeseeable accidents are given in my very project and constitute its meaning. Thus the unexpected puncture which upsets my projects comes to take its place in a world pre-outlined by my choice, for I have never ceased . . . *to expect it as unexpected.* And even if my path has been interrupted by something which I should never have dreamed of—like a flood or a landslide—in a certain sense this unpredictability was foreseen. Just as the Romans reserved in their temple a place for unknown gods, so in my project a certain margin of indetermination was created "for the unpredictable," and this was done not because of experience with "hard blows" or an empirical prudence but by the very nature of my project. . . .

. . . every project of freedom is an open project and not a closed project. Although entirely individualized, it contains within it the possibility of its further modifications. Every project implies in its structure the comprehension of the *Selbstandigkeit* of the things in the world. This perpetual foreseeing of the unforeseeable as the margin of indetermination of a project which I am enables us to understand how it is that an accident or a catastrophe, instead of surprising me by its unknown or its extraordinary quality, always overwhelms me by a certain quality which it has of "being already seen—already foreseen." . . . There is nothing which astonishes in the world, nothing which surprises us without our determining ourselves to be surprised. The original theme of astonishment is not that this or that particular thing exists within the limits of the world but rather that there is a world in general; that is, that I am thrown among a totality of existents thoroughly indifferent to me. This is because in choosing an end, I choose to have relations with these existents and because these existents have relations among themselves. I choose that they should enter into combination to make known to me what I am. Thus the adversity of which things bear witness to me is pre-outlined by my freedom as one of its conditions, and it is on a freely projected meaning of adversity in general that this or that complex can manifest its individual co-efficient of adversity. . . .

. . . I am absolutely free and absolutely responsible for my situation. But I am never free except *in situation*.

Man thus escapes determinism as he acts upon his projects, with their inevitable accompaniment of risk and indeterminacy. Some people perceive themselves in situations bounded entirely by indeterminacy and nothingness. Other people find themselves in situations bounded by the Transcendent, or by some "mystery" at the verge of the abyss.

GABRIEL MARCEL

The Philosophy of Existentialism

Being is—or should be—necessary. It is impossible that everything should be reduced to a play of successive appearances which are inconsistent with each other ("inconsistent" is essential) or, in the words of Shakespeare, to "a tale told by an idiot." I aspire to participate in this being, in this reality—and perhaps this aspiration is already a degree of participation, however rudimentary.

Such a need, it may be noted, is to be found at the heart of the most inveterate pessimism. Pessimism has no meaning unless it signifies: it would surely be well if there were being, but there is no being, and I, who observe this fact, am therefore nothing.

As for defining the word "being," let us admit that it is extremely difficult. I would suggest this method of approach: being is what withstands—or what would withstand—an exhaustive analysis bearing on the data of experience and aiming to reduce them step by step to elements increasingly devoid of intrinsic or significant value. . . .

A philosophy which refuses to endorse the ontological need is, nevertheless, possible; indeed, generally speaking, contemporary thought tends towards this abstention. But at this point a distinction must be made between two different attitudes which are sometimes confused: one

which consists in a systematic reserve (it is that of ag-
nosticism in all its forms), and the other, bolder and
more coherent, which regards the ontological need as the
expression of an outworn body of dogma. . . .

The former appears to me to be purely negative: it is
merely the expression of an intellectual policy of "not
raising the question."

The latter, on the contrary, claims to be based on a
positive theory of thought. . . . I shall only note that it
seems to me to tend towards an unconscious relativism,
or else towards a monism which ignores the personal in
all its forms, ignores the tragic, and denies the transcendent, seeking to reduce it to its caricatural expressions
which distort its essential character. I shall also point out
that, just because this philosophy continually stresses the
activity of verification, it ends by ignoring *presence*—
that inward realization of presence through love which
infinitely transcends all possible verification because it
exists in an immediacy beyond all conceivable media-
tion. . . .

Thus I believe for my part that the ontological need
cannot be silenced by an arbitrary dictatorial act which
mutilates the life of the spirit at its roots. It remains true,
nevertheless, that such an act is possible, and the conditions of our life are such that we can well believe we
are carrying it out; this must never be forgotten.

These preliminary reflections on the ontological need
are sufficient to bring out its indeterminate character and
to reveal a fundamental paradox. To formulate this need
is to raise a host of questions: Is there such a thing as
being? What is it? etc. Yet immediately an abyss opens
under my feet: I ask these questions about being, how
can I be sure I exist?

. . . Here . . . which I would call the ontological
status of the investigator assumes a decisive importance.
Yet so long as I am concerned with thought itself I seem
to follow an endless regression. But by the very fact of
recognising it as endless, I transcend it in a certain way:
I see that this process takes place within an affirmation

of being—an affirmation which I *am* rather than an affirmation which I *utter*: by uttering it, I break it, I divide it, I am on the point of betraying it . . .

MAURICE MERLEAU-PONTY

Sense and Non-Sense

Metaphysics begins from the moment when, ceasing to live in the evidence of the object—whether it is the sensory object or the object of science—we apperceive the radical subjectivity of all our experience as inseparable from its truth value. It means two things to say our experience is our own: both that it is not the measure of all imaginable being in itself and that it is nonetheless co-extensive with all being of which it can form a notion. This double sense of the *cogito* is the basic fact of metaphysics: I am sure that there is being—on condition that I do not seek another sort of being than being-for-me. When I am aware of sensing, I am not, on the one hand, conscious of my state and, on the other, of a certain sensuous quality such as red or blue—but red or blue are nothing other than my different ways of running my eyes over what is offered to me and of responding to its solicitation. Likewise, when I say that I see someone, it means that I am moved by sympathy for this behavior of which I am a witness and which holds my intentions by furnishing them with a visible realization. It is our very difference, the uniqueness of our experience which attests to our strange ability to enter into others and re-enact their deeds. . . . Metaphysics is the deliberate intention to describe this paradox of consciousness and truth, exchange and communication, in which science lives and which it encounters in the guise of vanquished difficulties or failures to be made good but which it does not thematize. From the moment I recognize that my experience, precisely insofar as it is my own, makes me accessible to what is not myself, that I am sensitive to the world and to others, all the beings which objective thought placed at a distance draw singularly nearer to me. Or, conversely, I recognize my affinity with them; I am nothing but an ability to echo them, to understand them, to respond to them. My life seems absolutely individual and absolutely universal to me. This recognition of an individual life which animates all past and contemporary lives and receives its entire life from them, of a light which flashes from them to us contrary to all hope—this is metaphysical consciousness, whose first stage is surprise at discovering the confrontation of opposites and whose second stage is recognition of their identity in the simplicity of *doing*. . . .

Doing, acting, choosing—these are the watchwords of existential thinking and existential education. The world remains open; the world remains strange; and history is possibility. The teacher, then, may conceive himself to be a metaphysician, an ironist, an artist; but, first and last, he must conceive himself as a living man.

ALBERT CAMUS

Resistance, Rebellion, and Death

The artist takes from history what he can see of it himself or undergo himself, directly or indirectly—the immediate event, in other words, and men who are alive today, not the relationship of that immediate event to a future that is invisible to the living artist. Judging contemporary man in the name of a man who does not yet exist is a function of prophecy. But the artist can value the myths that are offered him only in relation to their repercussion on living people. The prophet, whether religious or political, can judge absolutely and, as is known, is not chary of doing so. But the artist cannot. If he judged absolutely, he would arbitrarily divide reality into good and evil and thus indulge in melodrama. The aim of art, on the contrary, is not to legislate or to reign supreme, but rather to understand first of all. . . .

And the aim of education? The existential thinker would say it is the same.

EPILOGUE

Questions inevitably arise. Existential writers are telling about their own personal responses to their own existence; they seem to be addressing other single creatures, particularly those attuned to their own subjectivity. Their concerns seem in one sense cosmic, in another sense desperately private. What do these have to do with the humdrum, organized life of classroom and lecture hall?

"You must change your life," Rilke once wrote, referring to experience with a work of art. Perhaps this is what the existential writer demands of the one who encounters him; but, if so, it must be personal life that is to be changed, not professional attitudes or orientations. The teacher—or the teacher-to-be—who pays heed must acknowledge somehow that his effectiveness, like his authenticity, depends to some degree upon the nature of his personal commitment. He must acknowledge that he cannot live in two domains—private and professional. If he has chosen himself to teach, then teaching must become *his* "fundamental project," his means of creating himself.

There remains the question of the *use* of such an insight. What does the decision to change one's life, to recommit oneself, have to do with what is now becoming known about the teaching-learning enterprise? How is it possible for existential insights to be built into the cognitive structure that the contemporary educator needs? Is it not the case that preoccupation with one's own inwardness will distract one from theory and rational controls?

If there is an answer, it can only be found when the person engaged in teaching seeks it in the actual situations of his life. An answer can only be meaningful when an *individual* arrives at it, an individual who can maintain the vantage point of one intentionally and immediately involved.

In truth, this is the vantage point required for clarifying most educational issues; and it is one too seldom taken. Too often, those who study the subject called "education" consider the processes and phenomena to which that word refers from without. They talk and write about "education" without any feeling of responsibility for what happens in any particular school. This may be appropriate for behavioral scientists, asked to describe the institutional patterns of a society or a group. It may be appropriate, on occasion, for historians and anthropologists.

But the situation of the teacher is as different from these as is the situation of the psychotherapist from that of the statistician. No matter how deliberately, how rationally the teacher guides what happens in his classroom, he personally is involved in it; and almost everything that occurs is affected by his presence there, by his moods and gestures, his expectations and explanations, his responses to those who are trying to learn. A "true," a reliable account of a teaching situation is the one presented from that vantage point, since it is the only one which can take intention into account—the intention of the living individual who is making choices, guiding discoveries, identifying possibilities.

There is a sense, then, in which both an "inner" and an "outer" vision is required. There is a sense in which the multiple facets of the educational process can be described from both perspectives; and when one perspective is taken, the facets seen from the other need be neither eroded nor denied. This means that, if one looks existentially upon the act of teaching—taking choosing into account, and freedom, and being *there*—the strategies devised by the teacher, the tasks he identifies as learning, or the materials he uses, continue to be as consequential and "real" as the physical classroom itself.

It is important to see this after reading existential literature. It is important, too, to think about the ways in which the subjectivity of the teacher may sustain his rationality, and about the ways in which a decision to be intelligent may sustain the struggle to be.

There is no reason, therefore, to suspect dichotomy; there are no necessary either/ors where human existence is concerned. The person who is a teacher may be conscious of his own condition, his own fearful freedom, and at once behave strategically at his work. The major difference between the "inner" and the "outer" lies in the relationship between idea and action in each dimension: one can draw logical inferences from theory for teaching behavior; one can define no implications for behavior in general from encounters with existentialists.

Since this means that we can posit no existential theory or philosophy of education, given or derived, it leads us back to our earlier question: how can we put our encounters to use? We have said that they may move the one who experiences them to renewed consciousness of his life's commitment, but this gives little promise of help, if help is conceived in general, prescriptive terms. The very notion of doctrine is excluded by the existential view. Prescription is excluded by the centrality of free choice. All we can say is what we said originally: if the individual who engages with existential writers is committed to the study of teaching and learning, and to the action which is teaching, he—or she—cannot but see education with new eyes when the reading is, for the moment, done.

And he—or she—can say how it looks after such an experience. Saying, such a person will at least indicate possibilities; and these possibilities may be acted upon by others who are seeking their own vision, their own enhanced awareness of themselves. This, it is hoped, will be the response to the commentaries placed among the foregoing readings. They are personal statements; they are neither deductions nor explications. They were written by one committed to being an educator, and so they have to do with education. But there still exists a world of things to say by the others, the many others, who may also choose to see.

Education, for many people, signifies a process of unfolding. The teacher's function, according to this view, is to make it possible for a child to realize his inborn potentialities, to actualize himself. Whether this is accomplished through deliberate efforts to arouse activity in the child, through the creation of an "educative" environment, or through some non-directive, intuitive approach, the objective is to permit the child to be whatever he has it in him to be. Those who conceive education in this way are those who prize spontaneity and difference, who hope to see a society composed of autonomous individuals, each of whom is committed to his own form of "excellence," all of whom are committed to a common good.

Education, for other people, signifies a process of rearing, of deliberately cultivating certain tendencies and discouraging others, depending upon what the cultural situation demands. The end of education so conceived is productive membership. The individual, properly reared, is equipped with the beliefs, skills, and techniques of thought which are meant to enable him to function adequately in his society. Achieving identity through participation in a culture and a heritage, he is ready to take his place in history. He has been taught, and presumably he has chosen, to act upon values which are communal, to forge in the midst of the many a significant personal life.

Education, for still others, signifies a course of initiation, through which young people are enabled to form the inchoate world of experience by means of the cognitive disciplines and the arts. The primary aim of education, in this view, is to liberate and sensitize young minds for cognition, vision, innovative thought. Properly taught, they will be expected to find pleasure in the subject matters that they will discover as their store of concepts grows and as their perspectives diversify and expand. And, although there will never be an end to their learning, they will be increasingly free and competent when it comes to ordering the substance of their lives.

The emphases shift as the generations pass and the earth turns. In all the important views of education, however, there is concern for the diffuse and multiple energies of the child. There is an interest, always, in the ways in which particular children may be stimulated to learn, in the curricula conducive to the patterns of growth considered valuable, and in the human world where the child will perform his adult tasks.

Clearly there are points of contact between each of these views and the responses aroused by the readings in this book. The integrity of the individual seems central to the view of education as unfolding. Being-in-the-world seems focal to the conception of education as rearing. And those who speak in terms of initiation are concerned with the learner's own responsibility for enlarging his vision and achieving growth.

None of these views, however, seems to summon up an image of the contemporary learner under the conditions of the present age. An encounter with existentialism makes such an imaging crucial for the person choosing himself to be a teacher at this time. The import of "this time," this particular historic moment, cannot be overlooked by the one who tries to see, even for an instant, through an existential glass.

It is *now* that our teaching is to be carried on, *now*, in the second half of the twentieth century. Conscious of the now, we may consider the very process of learning to be a rebellion against the forces which abstract and depersonalize. How, having read what we have read, can we forget what these forces have done to persons? How can we overlook what it means to resign oneself to a "crowd"? We see the individual struggling against the incursions of that crowd when he is a child and when he is grown. We see ourselves as teachers goading him on to "live dangerously" for his own sake, to combat inertia, to take the risks of growth. We see a student choosing to learn only as he commits himself to achieve his own reality, only as he defines his own "fundamental project," which is to act on his own possibilities.

The principle of mere unfolding begins to seem alien, once we confront the obstacles to being: the neutrality of nature, the essential indifference of the world. But we agree that each person must act upon his own possibilities, recognizing them as such. And he must be held responsible for his choice. He must ache to learn and to grow; and we must welcome his aching and unease. We must welcome the anguish he may feel, the guilt before his own refusals. There may be no sin so great as the sin of refusing to become, to be.

Responsible as we are for indicating possibility to him, we know that all we can do is enable him to will his own freedom and make his own choices. As teachers, we can provide curricula rich enough and diverse enough to excite all sorts of youngsters to attempted mastery. We can provide a ground for the "lurch" into teachability. When the individual learner begins moving restlessly, when he shows signs of abandoning formlessness and pre-reflective "slime," we can acknowledge each small advance he makes, so long as it is in the direction decided on by the youngster himself with the knowledge that he is being given his single chance on earth, that he will never pass this way again.

No matter how many students we have in our classrooms, we will not (having read what we have read) treat the individual as a "specimen." We will not objectify him or make him an object of study, even when we consult the assessments made of what he can do or what he has achieved. Knowing we are "other" with respect to him, we can nonetheless work for encounters with him—for the sake of his authenticity and our own.

We may succeed in entering an "I-Thou" relationship; we may dare to engage in dialogue with him and open ourselves to him as he opens himself to us. But we recognize, if we do this, that we are opening the way to tensions and anxieties, the disquietude that is so essential to growth.

We engage in relationships with young people, as with our contemporaries, in an effort to release the "single one." No one of our pupils is likely to live as an isolate, not in a world where others are always present; therefore we must make it somehow possible for each to live among those others while remaining authentically himself. He will be threatened constantly by the appraising "look," the stare that demeans and objectifies. His sincerity will be put to the test by the social games he and others must continually play. But classroom situations can be made occasions for strengthening his will to be authentic and free—if, that is, we who teach are willing to open ourselves sufficiently to be *present* there. If we are, if we can stand forth as existing selves while we teach, we can transform our classrooms into exemplary places where presentness and objectivity coexist.

We can exert ourselves to see through the eyes of the student "other," to take his perspective, his vantage point, even while we concern ourselves deliberately with objective things. We can, while working with the structures of subject matters, with the tasks that must be performed if our students are to learn, create an atmosphere of intersubjectivity. Tranquillity will not pervade such an atmosphere; the members of the class will not be put at ease. But neither will they be dealt with as objects, cases, specimens. Engaged as subjectivities as well as minds, they may discover the possibility of being with others and at the same time being themselves. They may learn that one is not doomed to be a thing in an objective, public domain, so long as one ventures out of coolness and separateness—so long as one rebels through questioning and forming, and insists on the right to grow.

Continuing to look through an existential glass, we find ourselves affirming the priority of consciousness at every moment of classroom life. It is, however, when we are attending to the fundamental work of teaching—arousing our students to inquiry—that we pay particular heed to that priority.

As we have seen, the child does not begin as a reflective creature. Rather, he relates to the world around him by means of his feelings and moods. He gives rudimentary meaning to things as he touches them and uses them. It is only as he learns to investigate it, to symbolize it in language, to "tell about" what he finds, that he imposes significance upon his environment. Once he begins to do this intentionally, he begins to break with the habitual and familiar; and he continues to break with the "given" as he frees himself for more diversified forming and as he learns to create the orders within which he can decently live.

As teachers, we became concerned not with *what* he knows but with *how* he comes to know, how the truths of the world and of consciousness are revealed to the "single one." We endeavor to keep ourselves and the child in touch with concrete life situations, since these represent the dimensions of the world-to-be-known. The individual comes to know as he achieves appropriate relationships with various aspects of his life situations; sometimes he relates himself as a scientist would to empirical phenomena; sometimes, as an artist would to forms which are deeply felt; sometimes, as a statesman would to the practical strategies of life.

This, too, is an area where dichotomies have no place. The object is not to choose between the intuitive and the rational-empirical, the aesthetic and the discursive, the emotive and the logical. Nor is it to establish priority for one way of knowing above all others. The teacher's concern must be for the way in which each student chooses his relationship with the various situations which arise; for if knowing is conceived as a relationship with a variety of concrete situations, the student will not be likely to take refuge in the propositions of "pure" reason and disembodied intellect. As seeker, as knower, he will be participant. He will construct orders and define meanings as he chooses to do so, as he acts upon and challenges his world.

Only as he chooses can he achieve a continuity of identity and a continuity of knowing. As a free individual, he must take his choices seriously and commit himself in the space he discovers between his limitations and his possibilities. If not, he will flounder "in the possible"; and the project which is his selfhood will become abstract and finally meaningless.

And so we who teach must give him "care" and intense concern. We must foster the freedom that he can attain as he moves dialectically between necessity and fulfillment, between the ineradicable qualities of his particular situation and the thus-far-unrealized capacities which are his. "Cast into the world" though he may have been, the individual has grown up in situations: of slum life, perhaps, of poverty, of parental dominance, of rootlessness. These need not determine him; they certainly do not define him; but they do compose the frame of reference in which his becoming must take place. He cannot make decisions in a vacuum; he cannot define his possibilities if he is unaware of limitations, of necessities.

He is caught in a dialectical movement, therefore, when he acts to learn and to create himself; and, inevitably, he will feel strain, he will suffer as he struggles to become. It is in that suffering, however, that he experiences the pain of willing and the intensity of consciousness which make a person feel himself to be an existing creature—sharply and painfully alive. And it is in the midst of such intensity that he will be moved to shape values as he lives, to create his "ethical reality."

Values may be arbitrary at some level, but they do not appear in a vacuum. The individual must feel himself to be a distinctive person, confronting negations, caught up in the situations which give content to his life. These situations, as we teachers know, are social and political; they are economic, recreational, religious; occasionally they are situations of love, passion, friendship, faith. And they are, always, temporal situations, conditioned by history and by transiency.

The meaning and the impact of such situations are determined by the individual who encounters them; and one of our commitments as teachers is to enable him to confront them and choose appropriate action when he does. This is another reason for teaching for the widest, most varied perspectives: the young person must be equipped to perceive himself imaginatively in multiple predicaments, against diverse backgrounds. He must be, as he learns, a seeker and a wanderer. He must be adventurous enough to break repeatedly with the conventional. He must image himself in the great reaches of time and in continually expanding space. And at climactic moments of decision, he must experience the "boundary situations," where he can confront the "Encompassing," or the unanswerable, or non-being, or the absurd.

On the one hand, this implies a necessity for the most "general" curriculum, at least in the early years of his life. If he is to relate himself to novel situations as he chooses his future, he must experience himself thinking now like a scientist, now like an artist, now like a strategist. He must be given opportunities to manipulate, to experiment, to hypothesize, to test. He must be offered possibilities, as well, for knowledgeable appreciation of art forms, for vicarious identification with literary figures. He must find himself occasions for appropriating ideas, ideals, visions of possibility from a heritage made contemporary with him.

On the other hand, the prospect of confronting strange situations ought to lead the individual student to rehearse encounters with absurdity. He must not be protected, therefore, from inequity, injustice, suffering, and death—nor from the frequently unanswerable questions to which they give rise. It is only as he confronts the existence of "plague," only as he intensifies his own consciousness of "dread," that he may be moved to commitments which are ethical.

We cannot indoctrinate him with moral regulations if we intend to nurture his freedom. We cannot impose a ready-made value system upon him if we want him to choose himself. We can, however, open the way to the confrontations which will require him to make choices, choices involving conceptions of "good" and "right." In his freedom, then, he will shape a conscience for himself; he will construct a morality. And if the situations of his life (including the ones we have made) permit him to act on the possibilities he perceives, he will commit himself to the moral ideals that he has chosen. Taking responsibility, he will have achieved the hope of meaning at that point; he will have become a rebel for a cause.

This approach to the individual learner is one possible response to engagement with existential thought, as we have said. It is, significantly enough, an approach congruent with the emphasis on intellectual discovery, on autonomous learning, on "becoming" in current educational discussions. In the great centers of curriculum reform, in the offices of subject-matter specialists, in the laboratories of psychologists of learning, men are recognizing that learning is a function of teaching—and that it is an internal process conducted idiosyncratically by an individual. Even where teaching machines are being built and installed, the talk is of differential rates of speed, distinctive styles and rhythms of learning. There is anticipation of a computer center which will make "dialogue" possible for each student in the classroom, enabling him to move by means of his own questions, his own intentions, toward the kind of mastery possible for him.

The educational specialists, of course, have their eyes mainly on conceptual growth and on the subject matter appropriate to each level of development. They stress individual and developmental differences in the interests of efficiency, not because of an "I-Thou" concern. And the very nature of their investigations makes them consider the student as an abstraction, an object of study, rather than as a "fellow creature." This is wholly understandable. In situations where research takes place or experimentation, the existing human person has no place.

This does not mean that he can be obliterated. Surely it ought not to mean that his uniqueness is irrelevant in the other situations of life. As we have seen—as can be seen every day of our lives—this is precisely what young people are protesting, more vehemently than ever before.

There is a profound desire for recognition. There is a need for intense consciousness, for significant and moving experiences, and for the "courage to be" in a mute, indifferent world. Existential encounters cannot satisfy this need; but they may at least make it possible to affirm it. And they may liberate a teacher here and there for becoming and for choosing. If they do, they will serve the most important cause—the cause of life.

BIBLIOGRAPHY

The page numbers following the entries indicate the pages of the books from which the selections were taken.

Barnes, Hazel E. *Humanistic Existentialism: The Literature of Possibility.* Lincoln: University of Nebraska Press, 1959.

Barrett, William. *Irrational Man.* New York: Doubleday & Company, 1958.

———. *What Is Existentialism?* New York: Grove Press, 1965.

Blackham, H. J. *Six Existentialist Thinkers.* New York: Harper Torchbooks, 1959.

Bretall, Robert, ed. *A Kierkegaard Anthology.* Princeton, N.J.: Princeton University Press, 1947, pp. 33, 35, 102–107, 158–159, 193–194, 213–215, 287–288.

Buber, Martin. *Between Man and Man,* translated by Ronald Gregor Smith. Boston: Beacon Press, 1955, pp. 98–101, 200–203.

———. *I and Thou,* translated by Ronald Gregor Smith. New York: Scribner's, 1960, p. 131.

Camus, Albert. *The Myth of Sisyphus.* New York: Alfred A. Knopf, 1955, pp. 12–22.

———. *The Plague.* New York: Alfred A. Knopf, 1948, pp. 226–230, 231.

———. "Preface to *The Stranger.*" New York: Vintage Books, 1954.

———. *The Rebel.* New York: Alfred A. Knopf, 1954, pp. 229–232.

———. *Resistance, Rebellion, and Death.* New York: Alfred A. Knopf, 1961, p. 266.

———. *The Stranger.* New York: Vintage Books, 1954, pp. 151–154.

Dostoevsky, Fyodor. *The Brothers Karamasov,* translated by Constance Garnett. New York: Modern Library, 1945, pp. 289–291.

———. "Notes from Underground," in *The Short Novels of Dostoevsky,* translated by Constance Garnett. New York: Dial Press, 1945, pp. 46–47.

Grene, Marjorie. *Dreadful Freedom: A Critique of Existentialism*. Chicago: University of Chicago Press, 1959.

Heidegger, Martin. *Discourse on Method*. New York: Harper & Row, 1963, pp. 56–57.

———. *An Introduction to Metaphysics*. New Haven, Conn.: Yale University Press, 1959.

———. "What Is Metaphysics?" in *Existence and Being*. Chicago: Henry Regnery, 1948, pp. 329–343, 347–349, 355–356.

———. *What Is Philosophy?*, translated by William Klubach and Jean T. Wilde. New York: Twayne Publishers, 1958, pp. 83, 85.

Jaspers, Karl. *Man in the Modern Age*. Garden City, N.Y.: Anchor Books, 1957, pp. 24–29, 175–177, 210–211.

———. *Reason and Existenz*. New York: Noonday Press, 1955, pp. 79–80, 85, 91–92, 131–135.

Kafka, Franz. *Amerika*. Garden City, N.Y.: Anchor Books, 1946, pp. 37–38.

———. "Aphorisms," in *The Great Wall of China: Stories and Reflections*. New York: Schocken Books, 1946, pp. 264–273.

Kierkegaard, Soren. *The Journals*. New York: Harper Torchbooks, 1959, pp. 119, 251.

———. *The Point of View for My Work as an Author*. New York: Harper Torchbooks, 1962, pp. 27–28, 29.

———. *The Present Age*. New York: Harper Torchbooks, 1962.

———. *Sickness Unto Death*. Garden City, N.Y.: Anchor Books, 1952, pp. 168–170.

Kneller, George F. *Existentialism and Education*. New York: Philosophical Library, 1958.

Marcel, Gabriel. *The Mystery of Being*, Vol. I. Chicago: Henry Regnery, 1951, pp. 252–255.

———. *The Philosophy of Existentialism*. New York: Citadel Press, 1961, pp. 14–18.

May, Rollo, Ernest Angel, and Henri E. Ellenberger, eds. *Existence*. New York: Basic Books, 1959.

Merleau-Ponty, Maurice. *The Primacy of Perception*. Chicago: Northwestern University Press, 1964, pp. 5–7, 26–27.

———. *Sense and Non-Sense*. Chicago: Northwestern University Press, 1964, pp. 93–94.

Molina, Fernando. *Existentialism as Philosophy*. Englewood Cliffs, N.J.: Prentice-Hall, 1962.

Morris, Van Cleve. *Existentialism and Education*. New York: Harper & Row, 1966.

———. *Philosophy and the American School*. Boston: Houghton Mifflin, 1961.

Natanson, Maurice, ed. *Essays in Phenomenology*. The Hague: Martinus Nijhoff, 1966.

————. *Literature, Philosophy, and the Social Sciences.* The Hague: Martinus Nijhoff, 1966.

Nietzsche, Friedrich. *The Genealogy of Morals.* Garden City, N.Y.: Anchor Books, 1956, pp. 177–178, 254–256.

————. "Thus Spake Zarathustra," in Walter Kaufmann, ed., *The Portable Nietzsche.* New York: Viking Press, 1954, pp. 306–307.

Ortega y Gasset, José. *Man and People.* New York: Norton Library, 1957, pp. 109–110.

Reinhardt, Kurt F. *The Existentialist Revolt.* New York: Frederick Ungar, 1960.

Rilke, Rainer Maria. *Letters to a Young Poet.* New York: W. W. Norton, 1934, pp. 63–70.

————. *Selected Poems,* translated by C. F. MacIntyre. Berkeley: University of California Press, 1958.

————. *Sonnets to Orpheus,* translated by M. D. Herter Norton. New York: Norton Library, 1942, p. 113.

Roubiczek, Paul. *Existentialism: For and Against.* London: Cambridge University Press, 1964.

Sartre, Jean-Paul. *The Age of Reason.* New York: Bantam Books, 1959, pp. 137–138.

————. *Anti-Semite and Jew.* New York: Schocken Books, 1948, pp. 53–54.

————. *Being and Nothingness,* translated by Hazel Barnes. New York: Philosophical Library, 1956, pp. liii, 29–32, 49, 55–60, 252–255, 259–260, 507–509, 564–565, 610–611.

————. *Existentialism.* New York: Philosophical Library, 1947, pp. 26–39.

————. *The Flies.* New York: Alfred A. Knopf, 1946, pp. 121–122.

————. *Nausea.* New York: New Directions, 1959, pp. 56–58, 134–135.

————. *No Exit.* New York: Vintage Books, 1946, pp. 44–47.

————. *The Psychology of Imagination.* New York: Citadel Press, 1963, pp. 268–271.

————. *The Words.* New York: George Braziller, 1964, pp. 236–238.

Schrag, Calvin O. *Existence and Freedom.* Chicago: Northwestern University Press, 1962.

Thevenaz, Pierre. *What Is Phenomenology?* Chicago: Quadrangle Books, 1962.

Tillich, Paul. *The Courage to Be.* New Haven, Conn.: Yale University Press, 1952, pp. 81–82.

INDEX